Thomas A. Dwyer

Glimpses of the Brotherhood of Charity

Thomas A. Dwyer

Glimpses of the Brotherhood of Charity

ISBN/EAN: 9783743326828

Manufactured in Europe, USA, Canada, Australia, Japa

Cover: Foto ©ninafisch / pixelio.de

Manufactured and distributed by brebook publishing software (www.brebook.com)

Thomas A. Dwyer

Glimpses of the Brotherhood of Charity

GLIMPSES

OF THE

BROTHERHOOD OF CHARITY

BY

THOMAS A.ʹ DWYER, B. A.

WITH A PREFACE BY

REV. J. NILAN, D. D.

OF ST. PETER'S CHURCH, POUGHKEEPSIE, N. Y.

BOSTON, MASS.
PRESS OF THE HOUSE OF THE ANGEL GUARDIAN
1893.

TO THE EVER IMMACULATE VIRGIN MARY,
QUEEN OF HEAVEN
AND MOTHER OF
THE ORPHAN AND THE FRIENDLESS,
THIS BOOK IS LOVINGLY
DEDICATED BY THE AUTHOR.

CONTENTS.

CHAPTER I.

Introduction—Christ's Life a Life of Charity—He Draws Disciples to Him by Divine Love—The Great Napoleon's Tribute to the Charity of Christ—The Life of The Brothers of Charity Based on the Example of Christ. - - - - - - - - - 17-31

CHAPTER II.

Origin of the Congregation of The Brothers of Charity— A Short Sketch of Their Founder—Death of Father Bernard De Noter, the First Superior. - - - 33-40

CHAPTER III.

Brother Gregory Elected Superior General—The Founding of New Houses—Brother Gregory Resigns—Election of Brother Nicholas—The Advancement of the Congregation — Death of Brother Nicholas — Election of Brother Amedeus, the Present Superior General of the Congregation. - - - - - - - 41-60

CHAPTER IV.

Work of The Brothers of Charity in the House of The Angel Guardian — Father Haskins — Brother Justinian. - - - - - - - - - 61–85

CHAPTER V.

Rt. Rev. J. B. Fitzpatrick, First President of Trustees of the House of The Angel Guardian—Most Rev. J. J. Williams, Second President—Rev. M. P. Dougherty, First Secretary of the House of The Angel Guardian. - - - - - - - - - 86–104

CHAPTER VI.

Election of Brother Hilduward to the Office of Provincial—Continuation of the History of the House of The Angel Guardian—Election of Brother Wenceslaus—He is Transferred to Waterford, Ireland—Election of Brother Eusebius—Death of Brother Eusebius. - 105–122

CHAPTER VII.

Election of Brother Jude, Present Superior—The Rapid Advancement of the House of The Angel Guardian—The Amount of Good Being Done in the Cause of Orphanage. - - - - - - - - 123–131

CHAPTER VIII.

The Novitiate — The Interior Life of the Brothers of Charity. - - - - - - . - - 132–140

APPENDIX - - - - - - - - 141–144

PREFACE.

"The glory of Him who moves everything penetrates through the universe, and shines in one part more and another less."—Dante. Paradise, I.

In human conduct, this same glory of the first source of all activity shines with varied lustre in the different degrees of intellectual or spiritual work in which we are engaged. The active life appears to be the perfect condition in the present state of society. The value of the contemplative life must be measured by its actual fruits of beneficence. A life of mere contemplation is an impossibility.

The Brothers of Charity make it a necessary part of their striving after Christian perfection to perform the duties of the several offices in which they are employed. Beginning with the Brother Porter, who guards the door of the institution, the twelve different grades into which the members of the Congregation are ordained, afford ample opportunity for attaining the perfect Christian life, which every follower of Our Lord ought to seek. Perfect conformity to grace brings to each that perfection of which he is capable.

With the great and steady increase of wealth, there ought to be a proportionate growth of earthly comfort and social happiness. For a small number in the community, there is, undoubtedly, a larger share of worldly happiness than in former times. Those under the care of the Brothers of Charity are of the great multitude whose chances of enjoying the pleasures of life seem lessened by the wonderful increase of general prosperity. Hence, the work of education for advancement in life is of the gravest necessity. The practical training received in their institutions, imparting technical skill to meet the mechanical and artisan requirements, is an essential part of Christian instruction. The design of the Creator is evident in the progressive improvement of material nature, as well as in the advancement of the intellectual and moral order. One springs from the same creative act, as truly as the other; the development of each is of relative necessity, to illustrate the divine order in the complex system of creation.

In this respect, and in accord with the mission of the founder of Christianity, the work of the Brothers, to lift up the lowly, ought to inspire others with a like ambition. They serve the Master by saving His chosen ones,—the poor. Such service is that by which He commissioned His church to rule mankind. It was the sway gained by love of men. It triumphed, for it was divine. When failure succeeded, it was because human selfishness usurped the throne of divine love. Returning to the first supreme order of perfect law, society will find its regeneration; the Church will regain its lost supremacy; the human race will be the church, as its divine founder intended at its establishment.

Congregations, such as the Brothers of Charity, actuate the reign of Christ in the individual soul by exemplifying her perfect philanthropy. Where this is wanting, a moral and spiritual death ensues; the mere husk of the sacred fruit is often visible, and the false thus takes place of the true in the religious, as in the material order. A blind zeal can never aid any good cause; least of all the Christian cause. Hence the Brothers combine intellectual progress with artisan thrift.

REV. J. NILAN, D. D.

AUTHOR'S PREFACE.

How far that little candle throws its beams! So shines a good deed in a naughty world. — SHAKESPEARE.

His daily prayer, far better understood
In acts than words, was simply doing good.
— JOHN GREENLEAF WHITTIER.

To feel for and do much for others, and far less, or but little for ourselves, is the highest wisdom, fruitful of the greatest, most unalloyed happiness, and constitutes the best there is in human nature. — SIR PHILIP SYDNEY.

The men and women who unite in Brotherhoods and Sisterhoods, that they may the more honor Christ in devoting themselves unreservedly to the charity which He so nobly illustrated in every act of His life, are worthy of all praise, and of our most fervent prayers, and unstinted respect and love. And this duty has impelled me to write the book I now present to the public, setting forth the faithfulness to the dear Savior, of the noble Congregation of the Brothers of Charity.

The sole aim of the Brothers is to do good, and realize in the manner of their life and work, something of that love which brought to the ignominy of the Cross the Messiah, and gave to mankind freedom from the curse and bondage of the law of Sinai. Their trinity of vows, — Poverty, Chastity, Obedience,—leaves no chance for any other interests than those of a purely Christian life, to get their attention. The members of this Brotherhood have set themselves apart from the vanities and selfish pursuits of life, living wholly as Christ lived, namely, for the good of others. Their self-forgetfulness has scarcely any limit, and no sacrifice of personal comfort and pleasure is at any time too great for them to make in behalf of the good work they are ceaselessly engaged in doing. Of such a community of sincere Christian men, who can say too much, *yea, too much*, in their honor? And how voluminous soever might be a book recording the great benefit they confer on society, by their fidelity to their vows, which enables them the more deeply to impress their wholesome spiritual influence on all to whom they go, or who come to them, — such a book would be only a well deserved and fitting tribute to their sublime sense of Christian duty and love of their fellow creatures and the Catholic Church. Though I present no such a book at this present writing, I have been as voluminous as pressing cares and drafts upon my time would allow, hoping it may be possible for me at some point in the future to give the full attention to this noble and worthy Congregation of men, and their exalted virtues and wonderful achievements as heroes of the Church in the field of boundless charity, which they so pre-eminently merit. Who can properly estimate the vast importance of the service of such unselfish communities of Christians to the generations of human beings needing their care, which follow one another down through the ages? It is simply incalculable, and there is no adequate compensation for such service, and utter self-forgetfulness, but the love of Christ and

His Church, and the certainty of His recognition of all the good work done in His name and to His glory, in the day when He shall come to reward all who have followed Him, through every self-surrender, in righteousness and truth.

The writer begs leave to call the kind reader's attention to the fact that this little work is a labor of love. A desire to express his admiration for the noble Congregation of the Brothers of Charity, a tender love for the scenes amid which he has spent many happy days, and an earnest wish to attract more laborers into this portion of the Lord's vineyard have been the motives prompting this pleasing task.

> How few, like thee, enquire the wretched out,
> And court the offices of soft humanity;
> Like thee, reserve their raiment for the naked,
> Reach out their bread to feed the crying orphan,
> Or mix the pitying tears with those that weep!
> *   *   *   *   *   Think not the good,
> The gentle deeds of mercy thou hast done,
> Shall die forgotten all; the poor, the prisoner,
> The fatherless, the friendless, and the widow,
> Who daily own the bounty of thy hand,
> Shall cry to heaven for blessings on thee!
>   — JANE SHORE.

GLIMPSES OF THE BROTHERHOOD OF CHARITY.

CHAPTER I.

INTRODUCTION. — CHRIST'S LIFE A LIFE OF CHARITY — HE DRAWS DISCIPLES TO HIM BY DIVINE LOVE — THE GREAT NAPOLEON'S TRIBUTE TO THE CHARITY OF CHRIST — THE LIFE OF THE BROTHERS OF CHARITY BASED ON THE EXAMPLE OF CHRIST.

"You have heard that it hath been said: 'Thou shalt love thy neighbor, and hate thy enemy.' But I say to you: 'Love your enemies, do good to them that hate you, and pray for them that persecute and calumniate you, that you may be the children of your Father, who is in Heaven; who maketh His sun to rise upon the good and bad, and raineth upon the just and the unjust. For, if you love them that love you, what reward shall you have? Do not even the publicans this? Be you, therefore, perfect, as also your heavenly Father is perfect."— Matt. iv., 43, 44, 45, 46, 48.

"But," said Christ, "what think you? A certain man had two sons, and, coming to the first, he said: 'Son, go work to-day in my vineyard.' And he answering, said: 'I will not.' But afterwards, being moved with repentance, he went, and coming to the other he said in like manner. And he, answering, said: 'I go, sir,' and he went not. Which of the two did the father's will?"

"They say to him: 'The first.' Jesus saith to them: 'Amen, I say to you, that the publicans and the harlots shall go into the Kingdom of God before you. For John came to you in the way of justice, and you did not believe him. But the publicans and the harlots believed him; but you, seeing it, did not even afterwards repent, that you might believe him.'"—Matt. xxi., 28, 29, 30, 31.

What a delightful satisfaction it is to be helpful to others — to pass our lives going about doing good for the sake of the happiness we confer on the recipient of our benevolence, rather than for the desire of any selfish gain, or pecuniary advantage to ourselves. The world has never been, in any age, without some noble, pious, self-sacrificing souls, which made it a religious duty to care for the sick, and the suffering, and, in fact, for many of those who were incompetent to care for themselves. But it was reserved for Christianity to inspire men and women with the sublimest conception of the duties and compass of charity; which made such a degree of self-forgetfulness necessary to be practised, as never has failed to excite the wonder and astonishment of mankind in general, who are incapable of any self-forgetfulness whatever; and who live chiefly for what they can make out of each other by wholly selfish laws and customs; regarding every one as foolish who bases his life upon the high and holy principles of self-sacrificing charity, — a love that never faileth; that takes by the hand, and draws to its heart, the helpless and forsaken, and makes sunshine in souls where all before was darkness, hopelessness, and despair! And who but our dear

Savior, Christ, could inspire such heroic love and self-forgetfulness in the human heart and mind? He brought it with Him across the threshold of the temple, and into the lowly hovels of the poor. Christ, who, as the word, was in the beginning with God, and was God; who was the maker of all things; nor was anything made by any other; who, when evil wrought the fall of Adam, became by appointment of the Father, our gracious and voluntary Redeemer from the penalty of violated law, which was the terrible curse of eternal death! — who, in the fulness of time, came in the flesh, being conceived by our Lady, the Virgin Mary, through the power of the Holy Spirit, to be a sacrifice and atonement for our sins, as was foreordained in the councils of God, and promised mankind through the Covenant of Grace made by Him with Abraham, and confirmed unto Isaac and Jacob. How faithfully the Son fulfilled His mission upon earth by appointment of the Father, Holy Writ doth testify, and the Church doth unceasingly proclaim; while it has ever done honor to His name, and celebrated His priceless love and its dazzling glory. What a beautifully brief, divine, heroic, self-sacrificing life, was that of our dear Lord and Savior! Who can measure its magnitude, as a moral and religious force? How many millions of sad and despairing souls, since His death and resurrection, have been comforted and made happy by sincere faith in His atonement, authority and divinity! If the Son of God, yea, the very Father himself as a God-man, could patiently bear what was borne, as necessary for the sacrifice made for the redemption of man from the curse of sin, and of its penalty of eternal death, who should murmur at any suffering attendant upon this life, or think any sacrifice of vanity, pride, or personal ease, too great for them to make to the honor and glory of the Messiah? How majestic and faultless was His character; never yet has there been a charge of sin, or weakness, even, brought against it. The vilest, most reckless, and darkened-minded infidel who has lived at any time in this world, never yet has discovered anything with which to attack the sublime character of the Savior; nor has he dared, at the suggestion of an evil mind, to make an assault. At the early age of twelve, Jesus was found in the Temple with the Doctors of the Old Testament, or Jewish law, asking them questions, and attentively listening to their discourses, while He astonished them with the wisdom of His answers. Believed to have been brought up at the trade of His foster father, Joseph,—it was not until He was about thirty years of age that he entered upon His gloriously wonderful ministry, and completed that stupendous spiritual and moral work for the salvation of man from the curse of his own lawlessness,— work given Him to do, by the Father, as a voluntary sacrifice of Himself to the unyielding behests of law; beneath the rigorous exactions and oblivion of which man would have remained forever, but for the immeasurable love of God, as the Son, Redeemer, Prophet, Priest, King and Judge. Mystery of mysteries! Who can hope ever to penetrate it, — to harmonize it with human nature and natural law? Yet, before us it stands boldly out as the Rock of Ages,— an almighty and imperative truth!

Ascending from the river Jordan, where, at the baptism of John, the Holy Ghost descended upon him in the shape of a dove, a voice was heard coming from the open heaven, saying: "This is My beloved Son, in whom I am well pleased." Then it was He went forth on His mission of superlative love! Meeting with Simon Peter, at Lake Genesareth, after His forty days' sojourn and fast in the wilderness, and temptation by the devil, and His teaching in the synagogue of Nazareth, from which He was thrust by an enraged populace, provoked by His pretensions, independent spirit and bearing,— meeting with Simon, and feeling a close fellowship with sympathetic souls, He made a confident of him and his fellow-fishermen, James and John, whom He promised henceforth that they should catch men, in the place of fishes; and wrought for their benefit a surprising miracle, which confirmed their faith in Him as a superior being and teacher, with the divine and almighty power of forgiving sins; which caused the Pharisees, who believed God only had that power, to denounce Him as a blasphemer. But

He confounded these sceptics, and put them to confusion by the simple question: "Which is easier to say, 'Thy sins are forgiven thee,' or, to say, 'Rise up and walk?'" thereupon commanding the helpless, palsied man to take up his bed and go unto his own house; which he at once did, glorifying God, and effectually silencing the abusive Pharisees and Scribes; who watched Jesus continually, that they might find cause for accusing Him. It was at this time He took Levi into His confidence, a publican and a tax-collector, which led the Scribes and Pharisees to rail at Him because of this, and His attending a feast made by Levi, — Matthew, — in His honor. This assault drew forth from the adorable Savior that memorable speech, so pertinent and instructive, namely: "They that are whole need not a physician; but they that are sick. I came not to call the just and righteous, but sinners, to penance." They did not, nor could they, answer Him. In every attempt made throughout His entire ministry to convict Him of error, they signally failed, and marvelled at His mastery.

Having chosen from among His disciples twelve to be near His person and for special service, He delivered to them, and a great multitude, besides, a complete instruction in the moral and religious truths he wished, as Christianity, to found, and make effective for good and righteous living throughout the world! From that time onward, to His betrayal by Judas in Gethsemane, — a garden on the Mount of Olives,—and His trial, crucifixion and resurrection, He but reiterated, and in beautifully simple speech, enforced the morality and religion of His "Sermon on the Mount," as teaching to be accepted, and taken nearly and dearly to heart, by all who trust in Him and His Church throughout the ages.

A more charming illustration of Hope, Faith and Charity than is to be seen in the sublimely divine life of Jesus cannot even be imagined, and, last of all, realized. Well may such a life and character have drawn from Napoleon the Great, when in exile at St. Helena, the following grand tribute of admiration and love, — of faith in and devotion to the Godhead of Jesus, the Savior!

It may be found in Abbott's Memoirs of the wonderful hero and master of mankind: "April 21st, 1821. Said Napoleon to Dr. Antommachi, who attended him: 'You are an atheist, sir, and a physician. Physicians, dealing so exclusively with matter, are not given to believe in aught else. You hold yourselves above these weaknesses. I believe in God, and am of the religion of my father. Be an atheist, if you will and can, sir; but as for me, I was born a Catholic, and I fulfill all the duties which religion imposes, and seek all the solace which it administers.'"

The conversation at St. Helena frequently turned on the subject of religion. Of the divinity of Christ, Napoleon said to General Bertrand, who was a scoffing infidel: "I tell you, sir, I know men, and I say that Jesus Christ is not a man. Superficial minds see a resemblance between Christ, and the founders of empires, and the gods of other religions. That resemblance does not exist. There is between Christianity and other religions the distance of infinity! Everything in Christ astonishes me; His spirit overawes me,

and His will confounds me. Between Him and
whatever else in the world, there is no possible
term of comparison. He is truly a being by Himself. His ideas and His sentiments, the truths
which He announces, His manner of convincing,
are not explained, either by human organization,
or the nature of things. It is all to me a mystery,
which I can neither deny nor explain. His religion is certainly a revelation from an intelligence
far superior to man's. Its originality is profound,
creating a series of words and of maxims before
unknown. Nothing is borrowed from the sciences.
Nowhere can be found, but in Him alone, the
imitation or the example of His life. He is not a
philosopher, since He advances by miracles, and
from the commencement His disciples worshipped
Him. He persuaded far more by an appeal to
the heart, than any display of method and of
logic. Neither did He impose upon them any
preliminary studies, or any knowledge of letters.
All His religion consists in *believing*. In fact, in
His view, the sciences and philosophy avail noth
ing for salvation; since they teach us naught of

the mysteries of heaven or the laws of the spirit which He came to reveal. It is with the soul He has to do, and with that only; and to it He brings His gospel. Before Him the soul was as nothing. *Matter* and *Time* were the masters of the world! At His voice everything returns to order. Science and philosophy become secondary. The soul has reconquered its sovereignty. All the scholastic scaffolding falls, as an edifice ruined, before one single word,— Faith! What a master, what a word, which can effect such a revolution! If this is not the true religion, one is very excusable in being deceived, for everything in it is grand and worthy of God. I search in vain in history to find the similar to Jesus Christ, or anything which can approach the Word of God. There is nothing to be named to which I am able to compare it, or explain it. Here everything is extraordinary. The more I consider Holy Writ, the more I am assured that there is nothing there which is not beyond the march of events, and above the human mind. Even the impious themselves have never denied its sublimity, which inspires them with a sort of compulsory veneration. What happiness the Bible procures for them who believe it! What marvels those admire there who reflect upon it! Book unique, where the mind finds a moral beauty before unknown; and an idea of the Supreme Power, superior even to that which creation suggests! Who, but God himself, could produce that type, that ideal of perfection equally exclusive and original?

"Christ, having but a few weak disciples, was ignominiously pursued by the wrath of the Jewish priesthood, and crucified. He died in the contempt of the nation, abandoned and denied by His own disciples and apostles. Yet, as He promised, His cross has made Him dear to the hearts of multitudes in every generation, and simply by a mysterious energy in individuals scattered here and there in all parts of the world, having no other rallying sign than a common faith in its mysteries! What a unique, mysterious symbol! —the instrument of the punishment of the Godman. His disciples were armed with it. 'The Christ, God,' they said, 'had died for the salvation of men.' What a strife these simple words have raised around this standard of a divine love and religion! For three hundred years the spirit struggled against the brutality of sense; the conscience against despotism; the soul against the body; virtue against all the vices! In torrents the blood of Christians flowed, kissing the hands that slew them, as they died! Everywhere Christians fell, and everywhere they triumphed. The Cross has come to be a mighty and sublime power, assailed though it has been, and is, by the furious billows of rage, and the hostility of ages. And who, but God, for eighteen hundred years and more, has protected the Church from so many storms which have threatened to engulf it. Nowhere than in the Gospel and the Church, is to be found such a series of beautiful ideas, admirable moral maxims, which defile like the battalions of a celestial army, and which produce in our souls the same emotion that one experiences in contemplating the infinite expanse of the skies, resplendent on a summer's night with all the brilliance of the stars. Not only is our mind absorbed by the great truths of our religion, it is likewise enthralled; and the soul can never go far astray, with Holy Writ and the Church for its guide. Once master of our spirit, the faithful Gospel loves us. God ever is our friend, our Father, and truly our God. The mother has no greater care for the infant whom she nurses. What a proof of the divinity of Christ! With an empire so absolute, He has but one single end, the spiritual melioration of individuals, the purity of the conscience, the union to that which is true, the holiness of the soul! Christ speaks, and at once generations become His, by stricter, closer ties than those of blood, — by the most sacred, the most indissoluble of all unions! He lights up the flame of love which consumes self-love, and prevails over every love. The founders of other religions never conceived of this mystical love, which is the essence of Christianity, and is beautifully called *Charity*. In every attempt to effect this thing, namely, *to make himself beloved*, man deeply feels his own impotence. So that Christ's greatest miracle undoubtedly is the reign of charity."

Mankind can never be too grateful to Napoleon for this tribute to the love and charity of Jesus Christ. It is, as the great general says, the *charity* inculcated by the Christian Religion, which gives it pre-eminence over all other religions, and is its great and charming characteristic. And it is just this characteristic that gives the Brothers of Charity such an influence over the hearts of men. The more closely we study their sublime vocation, the more heroic it appears. At a time when many are saying that the power and usefulness of religious communities are declining, they, in their simple life, are exerting an influence that would have been noticeable in the brightest age of Christian history.

CHAPTER II.

Origin of the Congregation of the Brothers of Charity — A Short Sketch of Their Founder — Death of Father Bernard de Noter, the First Superior.

For the history of the Brothers of Charity, we must go back to the early part of the eighteenth century — see the frightful desolation caused by the French Revolution, behold Louis XVI., dethroned and imprisoned, and recall the dying groans of hundreds of beings, the innocent victims of wild fanaticism.

Nearly all Europe was engaged in war. Churches were in ruins, and almost every trace of religion obliterated; the faithful gathered into rude huts and stables, which were transformed into temples of the Most High. Priests offered the Holy Sacrifice in secrecy and fear. Such was the state of affairs when the Concordat of 1801 restored freedom to religious worship.

During this period, in that quaint old city of Belgium, called Ghent, a modest and unassuming priest, Father Triest, better known as the "St. Vincent de Paul of Belgium," might be seen, evidently in profound thought. With an aching heart he had experienced the miseries just described, and he sighed to heal the bleeding wounds caused by poverty and distress. He saw the youth of Belgium growing up, much in need of religious instruction, and he humbly begged God to inspire noble, generous souls to alleviate this distress.

As we study the history of the world, we find God continually making use of the weak to confound the strong. We read of young Saul defeating the great Amelec and delivering Israel from the hands of the enemy; Gregory XI., restored to the Eternal City through the instrumentality of a frail woman; a mere child, St. Rose of Viterbo, speaks, and the power of Frederick II., in all its might and magnificence, is shaken to its very foundation; and, lastly, we see rude fishermen chosen to preach the word of Eternal Life.

Father Triest was a chosen vessel of Divine Grace, whom Providence made use of to adorn the fair land of Belgium with a great number of charitable institutions, which soon wiped away the distress and misery left after the "Reign of Terror." He founded the Congregations of the Brothers of Charity, and the Brothers of St. John of God. Two congregations of women, known as the Sisters of Charity, and the Sisters of the Holy Childhood of Jesus, also claim him as their founder. To reach the more neglected of God's poor he established several societies of laymen, who visited the sick at their homes, caring for all with the most Christian charity.

Among the virtues which adorned the soul of Father Triest, Faith, Hope and Charity were the most conspicuous. His faith was always fervent, and showed itself in every act and deed of his life. With faith and submission to the authority of the Church, he carried on his work of advancing the communities he had founded. These communities were organized in such complete poverty that we might say their sole foundation was Divine Providence.

From this faith, so pure, so firm, so deeply rooted in the soul of Father Triest, sprang, as a leaf on a plant, that Hope in God which no power could shake, and which was his constant support in the hour of trial. He had a particular mission to erring souls. Like some great eagle sheltering its imperilled young from the rocky precipice, he spread the wing of hope over the sinner and brought him back to Christ; or like his Divine Master, who refused to cast a stone at the poor, sinful woman in the gospel, he sought to raise the fallen one by words of hope and comfort. This life of loving service won the hearts of those to whom he ministered. His strength lay in his ardent hope in God.

In the soul of Father Triest were united, in the sweetest harmony, the love of God, and the love of his neighbor in and for God. It was the glorious sun of his charity, that filled the soul of the cold and hardened sinner, with the warmth of God's

VERY REV. CANON DeDECKER.

love and mercy. That mode of conduct which he himself practised, he desired to be observed by others. For he wished to see those who were called to a life of perfection marching to it gaily, and not with sad faces and heavy hearts. He never wearied of recommending the practise of charity, to the members of his beloved congregations. All were persuaded that no one loved them as did this true Father.

The Congregation of Brothers to which he gave the sweet name of "Charity," and with which this brief history is concerned, has for its object the sanctification of its members, by the practise of works of charity. These works chiefly consist in caring for the sick, the old and insane, orphan and friendless boys, and the blind.

The foundation of such a Congregation in Europe during those stormy days of the French Revolution was a daring undertaking, and doubtless provoked much comment among the idle and curious. But like all the other good works founded by Father Triest, the Congregation of the Brothers of Charity made rapid progress, and spread itself all over Belgium, and, after fifty years of existence, it crossed the mighty ocean and brought its gospel of Charity and good will to a new continent.

But in these early days only God, who saw the hard labors of this little band of Brothers, could have any idea of the wonderful growth with which the small beginning was to be blessed.

The first Superior-General of the Congregation was Father Bernard De Noter. He was a man of solid piety, and gifted with rare energy. God had chosen him to be the first superior, and the support of the Congregation during its days of infancy, — days that were filled with trials and hardships which required a heroism approaching the sublime to withstand and endure. So thick and fast did bitter trials succeed each other, that the first companions of Father De Noter grew sick with discouragement, and abandoned the Congregation just a few months before their term of probation expired. Father De Noter, all undaunted, remained faithful to his vocation, and, with the help of the venerable founder, he succeeded in recruiting new companions, who longed to lead a life of obscurity, humiliation and poverty, for the kingdom of heaven's sake.

After four years of severe trials, Father De Noter and three of his companions were admitted to their vows, on November 26th, 1811. Father De Noter consecrated the new Congregation to the Queen of Heaven. Tossed about like a fragile bark on the billows of time, the infant community was on the verge of dissolution, when God's protecting hand drew it out of danger. The meagre four grew into hundreds, and four years later the General was able to found a second house in Ghent for the care of the insane. In 1820 Father Bernard founded another house at Bruges, which is to-day the largest and most important institution of the Congregation. Later, in 1832, he went to Louvain and founded a school for the education of youth. This school, under the direction of the Brothers, is still flourishing, and has an average attendance of one thousand pupils.

Worn out with hard labor and a life spent in trials and hardships for the sake of the Divine Master, the day of rest and reward was at last drawing near for Father Bernard De Noter. It was seen that the Reverend Superior was suffering more than commonly; but his courage gave false hopes to the Brothers. The hand of death was upon him, and day by day he faded away. Finally the end came, on a bright June morning, in the year 1832. Four years later Canon Triest, the pious founder, followed the venerable Superior into eternity.

Father Aloysius succeeded Father Bernard; and Rev. Benedict Constantine De Decker, who had been coadjutor to Canon Triest in the management of the affairs of the Congregation, succeeded him in his office.

Thus passed away these two heroic souls. Great during life, they were yet greater in death, and on their entrance into their heavenly home they might have said: "We have glorified Thee upon earth, we have finished the work which Thou gavest us to do." They were both magnificent instruments in the hands of God, whose designs are covered with an impenetrable veil, and are generally only known by their results.

Rev. Brother Amedeus,
Superior-General of the Brothers of Charity.

CHAPTER III.

BROTHER GREGORY ELECTED SUPERIOR-GENERAL — THE FOUNDING OF NEW HOUSES — BROTHER GREGORY RESIGNS — ELECTION OF BROTHER NICHOLAS — THE ADVANCEMENT OF THE CONGREGATION — DEATH OF BRO. NICHOLAS — ELECTION OF BRO. AMEDEUS, THE PRESENT SUPERIOR-GENERAL OF THE CONGREGATION.

Under the direction of the Rev. Canon De Decker, and the generalship of Father Aloysius, the number of houses belonging to the Congregation was increased by the new foundations of The Strop, (the school of the Biloque) in Ghent, St. Charles' Institute in Antwerp, and the blind asylum, known as Van Caneghem, in Ghent.

At a general chapter held in the year 1862, Brother Gregory, Superior of the Royal Institute of the Deaf, Dumb and Blind in Brussels, was elected General Superior. During the three years of his administration, and under the direction of Rev. Canon Deporte, who had succeeded Canon Decker, as Rev. Father of the Congregation, the new houses of Selzaete, Ziekeren, St. Trond were established. The Deaf and Dumb Institute of Ghent, which until now had formed one of the dependencies of The Biloque, was transferred to Roeighen (Ghent) and became a part of the newly built institute. It was also under the administration of Brother Gregory that the first institution abroad,— that of Montreal,—was founded. This institution, which is now the mother house of the American Province, was governed by the lamented Brother Eusebius, first provincial in America, of whom we shall speak later.

In October 1865, Father Aloysius was re-elected to the office of General Superior. During the whole of his second term, he bent his energies to the maintaining and strengthening of the institutions. Owing to his advanced years and failing health, he shrank from the responsibility of founding new ones. He was zealous in preserving a spirit of simplicity, poverty and retirement; watchful to maintain the observance of the rule in its minutest points; attentive to procure the advancement of each member of the community in the solid virtue of humility. Finally, growing too feeble to bear the burdens of the responsible office, which he had filled so satisfactorily for the long period of thirty-six years, he asked to resign. The permission was granted him, and October 6th, 1871, the Chapter elected to the vacant office Brother Nicholas, who had been director of the school of The Biloque for over twenty-seven years.

The new general took up his task where his predecessor had left it, and devoted his labors to the perfecting of the various houses of the Congregation. He traced out a uniformity of method to be adopted in each institution.

During the short period of his administration he accomplished an incalculable amount of good. Fraternal charity was the constant theme of his discourses to his brethren. In the government of the various houses, he regulated everything with great wisdom; even the smallest details gave evidence that the spirit which presided there was inspired. Here we may note that it was during his administration the Brothers took charge of The House of The Angel Guardian in Boston. The foundation of this institution and its history will be treated in another chapter.

On August 20th, 1876, the summons of death was again heard, and Brother Nicholas laid down the burden of life, as cheerfully as he would have relinquished his charge, at the voice of his superior. The Chapter assembled and elected Brother Amedius, Superior General, who is still at the head of the Congregation; young, strong, and gifted with high intellectual endowments, he guides the destiny of his flock with such zeal and success, that it should not be considered an indiscretion if his name were inscribed here in golden letters. During the seventeen years he has filled the office of Superior General, the Congregation has increased and multiplied in a manner that seems miraculous. New foundations have sprung up in England, Ireland, Canada and Belgium. The devoted General is constantly receiving requests to found new houses in various parts of Europe and America.

Brother Amedeus has decided views on education. He understands, perfectly, the system of teaching, and the best methods of conveying knowledge to the young untutored mind. In recognition of his services in the cause of education King Leopold of Belgium, in the year 1885, conferred on him the honored title of Grand Chevalier of The Order of Leopold; another title—Chevalier of Our Lady of The Immaculate Conception of Villa Viciosa—was conferred on him by the King of Portugal.

In his great work of advancing the young American Province, Brother Amedeus has found able assistants in Brothers Eusebius, Justinian, and Hilduard, who have each, in turn, filled the office of Provincial of the American Province. Through the instrumentality of Brother Amedeus the rules of the Congregation of the Brothers of Charity were approved by Rome in 1888, and received words of praise and admiration from the revered pontiff, Leo XIII.

The following addresses are the tributes Brother Amedeus received from the English speaking houses of the Congregation on the happy occasion of his silver jubilee, which occurred February 22nd, 1889. They are sufficient to show the esteem and love in which the Rev. General is held by the flock he guides so well:

ADDRESSES.

Most Honored and Venerated Father General:

Yes, dearly beloved Father in Christ, we, your affectionate children, rejoice indeed and join heart and soul with our cherished brethern on the Continent, in Ireland and America, and most joyfully celebrate your Silver Jubilee. That Jubilee of 25 years of indefatigable labor for God's glory and the good of souls. Oh! that it were given us to lift for a moment the veil of the past! What a history it would reveal! There, we would find the innumerable sacrifices you have made; the hardships you have undergone; the acute pains you have endured, brought on by long watches and excessive labor; the, humanly speaking, insurmountable obstacles you have overcome; and the most ardent prayers you have offered to God; all, all that the Congregation, our Mother, might increase her sphere of usefulness, and, above all, should continue in the spirit of her founder, the great, the good Canon TRIEST, that true disciple of her holy Patron Saint Vincent de Paul. There, we would find the secret of that constant extension of existing good works; those numerous creations of new institutions and their rapid development. But the crowning jewel of those most fruitful years is that priceless pearl, that inappreciable favor: the approbation of our constitutions by our Holy Father, Leo XIII, and the placing of our Congregation among those approved of by the Church. That, and that alone, should insure to you, beloved Father General, the love, veneration, and lifelong gratitude of your children.

But that love and gratitude you have long since won by your kindness, your fatherly affection, and your unwearied solicitude for the temporal and spiritual welfare of each one of us.

Ah! we know but too well our inability to repay

even a mite of what, after God, we owe to your kind and devoted heart; but we trust, and most fervently pray that our Blessed Lord will have pity on our weakness and take upon Himself the fulfilment of our obligations, by granting you peace and happiness here below, while waiting for the beautiful crown prepared for you in His glorious mansions above.

In the meantime, we will endeavor to prove by our fidelity to our holy Constitutions and Rules, our ardent desire to do all in our power to show our love and gratitude for you, most honored, most beloved, and most kind Father General.

Your grateful children in J.-C.,

FATHER LINUS AND THE BROTHERS
OF BUCKLEY HALL.

Rochdale, May, 1889.

JUBILEE SONG TO FATHER GENERAL.

BY THE BOYS OF BUCKLEY HALL, ROCHDALE.

Honor to you, we boys are singing,
    Vi-val-ler-al-ler-al-ler-a,
While still your jubilee bells are ringing,
    Vi-val-ler-al-ler-al-ler-a;
We truly wish you all the joys,
Giv'n to a Father by his boys.
    Vi-valler-aller-aller-a,
    Vi-valler-aller-aller-a,
    Vi-valler-aller-aller-a.

Then children haste your vows to pay,
    Vi-val-ler-al-ler-al-ler-a,
To our kind Father, O! let us say
    Vi-val-ler-al-ler-al-ler-a;
We will be brave, honest and true,
And obedient in our love for you.
    Vi-valler-aller-aller-a,
    Vi-valler-aller-aller-a,
    Vi-valler-aller-aller-a.

Receive, then, our joyous greeting,
    Vi-val-ler-al-ler-al-ler-a,
And our prayers to heaven ascending,
    Vi-val-ler-al-ler-al-ler-a;
That your golden jubilee
You may happily live to see.
    Vi-valler-aller-aller-a,
    Vi-valler-aller-aller-a,
    Vi-valler-aller-aller-a.

Very Dear and Reverend Father General:

We, your devoted children, the Religious of St. Patrick's Institution in this country, take this opportunity of your visit amongst us, with the deepest feelings of reverence and love, to congratulate you most heartily on the completion of your silver jubilee in our Congregation, at the head of which you have spent half of that time. Words fail us to convey to you all that our hearts feel; but we may assure you with perfect honesty that, while we have but seldom the happiness of being gathered round our common Father on Earth, the distance even at which we are living from his official residence lends a stronger degree to our affection for him, and causes us ever to look with unfeigned joy at the least chance we may have to welcome him amongst us, to show him our devotedness to his person, and make him happy with the certainty that he may have every confidence in this the most distant Institution and House of the Congregation in Western Europe, in the Belgium Province, where his will is law, and his desires the wishes of all the Religious serving this house.

We earnestly pray God and foster the fond hope that our dear Father General may long be spared to govern our Congregation, to see it extend, year by year, its sphere of usefulness, and to obtain an ample supply of candidates after his own heart.

May you, Father General, long be spared in health to govern our dear Congregation with that zeal and prudence and love of which you have for many years given to all so conspicuous an example.

We thank God, we thank you, dear Father, for the signal honor bestowed on us and the Congregation through your assiduous and sustained efforts with the Roman authorities, by which our Congregation has at length been recognized, and approved by the Holy Father; a work, we know, which has seriously affected your health and strength, but a work of love which lay nearest to your heart, and from which an untold degree of good is likely to spring.

Whether we look towards the East on our institutions in the country of the birth of the Congregration, or towards the far West of Canada and the United States, wherever we find an Institution of the Brothers of Charity, there we also find a House of the Congregation, and not only a House, but the Congregation itself; for now it is one and indivisible, and all its members are under one head everywhere under the sun, all united in a strong bond of love and affection for our dear Father General.

As you are, Father General, to embark once more upon a long and fatiguing voyage, and to face no less fatiguing labors in the far West, we beg of our good God to be with you, both on land and sea, in a special manner. May your travels be comfortable, your cares easy, your labors consoling, your return prosperous, and let us express the hope of once more seeing you, if possible, on your return home. May the Son of God bless and protect you, and give you the unspeakable consolation of seeing and leaving wherever your travels are to take you, everyone and everything in such order and such flourishing state as you yourself could wish and desire for the honor and glory of God and the credit of the Congregation.

Such, dear Father General, are the wishes of your devoted children

THE SUPERIOR AND BROTHERS
OF BELMONT PARK.

Waterford, Ireland, May, 1889,

Very Reverend and Dear Father Superior:

We, the members of the Community, beg to offer you our heartfelt congratulations on the occasion of your election for twelve years as Superior General of our Congregation. If one day spent in the House of the Lord; if the mere invitation to enter it seemed to the Royal Prophet a cause for joy and jubilation, how much more reason have we to rejoice at the long period which it was given you to spend in the service of God, especially when we consider what is implied in five and twenty years of religious life, and twelve of apostleship to the souls entrusted to your care. Those years have been years of generous self-sacrifice, of anxious solicitude, of bitter trials and many sufferings; but if the sowing has been in sorrow and the casting of seed amidst tears, the reaping has been in joyfulness; and today we may well congratulate ourselves and you that the tree you have planted, and the vine you have cultivated, have received wonderful increase, and borne plentiful fruit, and that the works you have undertaken truly flourish, being visibly blessed by the Almighty.

In our labors and merits you have a large share, as the first fruits belong to him who has tilled the soil and sown the seed. Justly may we rejoice and congratulate you, our Friend and our Father, on the great things it hath pleased the Lord to accomplish through you, during these twelve years of your generalship. Like the good shepherd, you walk before us in the path of duty, attracting by sweetness and charity and gentleness, correcting with meekness and mercy, leading by patience and example, strengthening the weak, confirming the strong, carrying the weary, comforting those who suffer, bringing back the straying, sustaining, aiding, consoling, pouring out the healing balm, binding up the wounds, being spent and spending for the sake of your flock, your time, your mind, your heart, your strength, your health and your life. Ever since Providence has placed you over us, you have been, to speak in the words of our Patron Saint Vincent, "the pattern of your flock from the heart," and your constant aim has been to make sweet the yoke of the Lord, and to render its burden light, winning all hearts by your loving kindness, in order to draw them to God.

We venerate in you the Pastor of whom the Lord says: "I will raise me up a faithful priest, and he shall do according to my heart and my soul, and I will build him a faithful house, and he shall walk all day before my anointed, and his path shall be the path of the just, a shining light going forwards and increasing even to perfect day."

We honor in you, above all, the edifying model of religious virtues, of earnest zeal for souls, of piety, of religious humility and brotherly charity.

Giving thanks to the Lord for the graces bestowed upon you, we will unite our prayers to your prayers, and repeat with all the fervor of our hearts

AD MULTOS ANNOS!

The Superior and Brothers of the House of Waterford. (Belmont Park.)

———

Reverend and Dear Father:

We, the pupils of the House of the Angel Guardian, respectfully bid you welcome to our Home. We know of no one having higher claims upon our affection. What we owe to the noble Brotherhood of Charity is more than can be described in words. At present we feel the paternal solicitude of its members every hour of our stay in this institution. Their guardianship stands as a perfect shield between us and evil. They watch our every step, note when we wander from the right path, and lovingly lead us back to it. Here, in the bosom of this happy family, untroubled by the discord and temptations of the streets, we learn how pleasant it is to be good. Should we forget it when we go out into the world, it will not be the fault of our good Superior, nor of his zealous Brothers in Religion. His and their labors in our behalf now, can have none but a beneficial influence upon our future. For all this we are indebted to the Brothers of Charity, and we would be guilty of ingratitude beyond all expression, were we not delighted to receive under our roof the man whom it has pleased the Almighty to call to the direction of their benevolent mission.

But in tendering you this greeting, dear Father Amedeus, we are not so foolish as to think, for a moment, that we are in the remotest sense doing you a favor. As Head of a Congregation of Religious, whose lives are vowed to the service of the poor and the afflicted, you carry your welcome with you wherever Christian heroism is esteemed. Much as the Congregation has done in this institution, we know it is but little in magnitude and character to what it has done elsewhere. While its purpose is to save, its members daily perform deeds more truly heroic than have ever been done upon the battlefields of history. We know of the unexampled services it renders to the aged, the poor, the sick, the blind, the deaf, the dumb, the insane and the criminal. To receive you, Father, to have under one roof with us the highest representative of this grand association, the projector and director of its Christlike works, is a high privilege for which we cannot feel too grateful.

Furthermore, we are aware that, distinguished as is the office you hold in the Congregation, you have still more distinguished it by your personal efforts.

In your own country, you have made the Congregation an impregnable barrier to the irreligious education of the day, winning thereby the respect alike of friends and foes.

Your sovereign has recognized your services to popular instruction, by creating you Chevalier of the Order of Leopold, and the confidence with which you have inspired the members of your Brotherhood has been manifested in their election of you to be the Superior General for the unusual period of twelve years. Of these testimonies of esteem, we do not need to be told that the latter is by far the most highly prized by you. The former you have accepted in loyal deference to the wishes of your king, and from motives, we are sure, untainted by human vanity. But never were spurs so nobly won, and never will there be so true a Knight. In the field selected for you by the pious Canon TRIEST, we know that you will be *sans peur et sans reproche*.

In welcoming you then, Father Amedeus, we are but honoring ourselves and partaking of the blessing which such as you, for whom so many prayers ascend to Heaven, must carry with you wherever you go. We could wish you to remain always with us, but as this cannot be, we trust your stay will be long, for we know it will be made most pleasant to you by our good friend and Father, our dear Superior.

THE PUPILS OF THE HOUSE
OF THE ANGEL GUARDIAN *(Boston)*.

The preceding pages have displayed before our readers a brief sketch of the early history of the

Congregation; they have seen the protecting hand of Providence ever extended over it and manifesting His love for it in manifold ways.

We will devote the next chapter to the House of The Angel Guardian, Boston, Mass., which is the only institution in the United States conducted by the Brothers of Charity.

FOUNDER OF THE HOUSE OF THE ANGEL GUARDIAN.

CHAPTER IV.

WORK OF THE BROTHERS OF CHARITY IN THE HOUSE OF THE ANGEL GUARDIAN — FATHER HASKINS — BROTHER JUSTINIAN

A tourist taking a survey of Boston, so celebrated for the grandeur of its buildings, the culture of its citizens, the magnificent beauty of its suburbs, beholds almost every indication of the highest degree of civilization and refinement.

As he gazes on the many institutions erected to relieve every kind of human misery, perchance his path may lead him to Vernon Street, which lies in one of the suburbs of the city; and no wonder that he asks, what is the purpose of the large brick building that stands out so conspicuously before him. Tarry, indulgent stranger, and hear the story this building has to tell. Your delay need not be long, for it has a history of only forty years to record.

Yes, not many years ago the suburb of Boston, bearing the name of Roxbury, now teeming with every evidence of progress, and every proof of industry, was considered a farming district. Time passed on, and one cold November day, on the site where now stands The House of The Angel Guardian, there stood a saintly priest viewing the barren spot, while before his mind's eye loomed up the great brick structure, which he was to build to shelter homeless and wandering waifs from the sin and crime of a great city.

For the history of this man's life we must take a further retrospect — see religion persecuted by a New England Knownothingism, listen to the lamentations of the devoted Ursuline nuns over the burning of their convent-home, and recall the cruelty and humiliation endured by noble Catholic priests, to spread the faith in New England. Ah! thus has cruel intolerance, in the name of liberty, drawn groans and denunciations from the very rocks of Massachusetts.

It is not far fetched to say, that even in this nineteenth century, any Catholic reared and educated in New England, can hear echoes that have been wafted from those days of cruelty and religious persecution — echoes of the prayers that ascended from the lips of fervent priests for the peace of God's church; groans wrenched from the honest, strong and manly Irish emigrant, who was denied the means of gaining bread for his little ones, on account of his loyalty to the Catholic faith; sighs of sorrow, the wailings of distress that commingling, ascended on the breeze, and cried to heaven for protection from this barbarous cruelty. Such was the condition of affairs, just previous to the conversion of Father Haskins to the Catholic religion. Gloomy, indeed, appeared the horizon of the faith the Master had led him to espouse; but when the same voice came nearer to his soul and called him to the priesthood, he entered with his whole strength into the spirit of his calling, and corresponded with the graces given him. No wonder, then, the result of his work should be what it is! What power one truly zealous priest may exert on mankind, is shown in the life of Father Haskins.

To write such an eventful life as that of Father Haskins, would require quite a volume, therefore, we will content ourselves with simply giving a short sketch of the history of this great and good man.

George Foxcroft Haskins, son of Thomas Haskins and Elizabeth Foxcroft, both descendants of the first settlers of New England, and firm adherents of the Episcopal Church, was born April 4, 1806, in his father's house, on the corner of Carver and Eliot Streets, Boston. At an early age he attended the school of Masters Webb and Payson, and later on the Boston Latin School, on School Street. Nothing of importance is recorded of his early childhood, except during the first years of his schooling, he conceived such a hatred of flogging, that he lost no opportunity in after life, as his numerous writings attest, of declaiming against this cruel practice.

At the age of sixteen, he entered Harvard College, and being an earnest student, he made a very successful course, and graduated with distinction in 1826; desiring to prepare for the church, he commenced the study of Theology under the direction of the Revs. Alonzo Potter and George W. Doane, both of whom were afterwards Protestant Episcopal bishops. It was about this time that Dr. Lyman Beecher visited Boston, and delivered a series of lectures against the Catholic Church. Mr. Haskins and his life-long friend, the late George W. Lloyd, Esq., attended these lectures, and with a view of hearing both sides, also attended a course given by Right Rev. Bishop Fenwick and Doctor O'Flaherty, able and eloquent preachers, and practical expounders of the Catholic faith. The seeds of truth were thus planted in his mind before he realized that the foundation of his Protestant convictions was loosened. Mr. Haskins at this time officiated as layman at South Leicester, every Sunday. On Feb. 8, 1829, he was ordained deacon of the Episcopal Church, by Bishop Griswold, and appointed Chaplain to the House of Industry, in Boston. In May, 1830, Mr. Haskins formed the acquaintance of Rev. Father Wiley, then attached to the old Cathedral on Franklin Street. This acquaintance led in time to his conversion to the Catholic faith. Their meeting happened as follows: There was in the House of Industry a poor old Irish woman, who, seeing her end approaching, begged for a Catholic priest. The superintendent answered the poor creature's request in these words: "Oh! I'll send you a priest as good as any of your Catholic priests;" and he sent her the Chaplain. Mr. Haskins went to the dying woman, who repeated to him her wish to see a Catholic priest before she died. The earnest manner in which she proffered her request moved his heart, and he said: "You shall have a priest; I'll go for him myself." He immediately went to the priest's house on Franklin Street, saw Father Wiley, told him his errand, and that he was a Protestant minister. The conversation which followed this announcement, induced Mr. Haskins to remark to a Protestant friend whom he met on leaving the house, that he would examine for himself certain things in Protestantism to which

Father Wiley had referred; and from that day his mind was bent on finding the truth. The old woman was visited by Father Wiley and received the Sacraments. When she saw the Protestant Chaplain again, she raised up her poor, weak hands, and, with tearful eyes, cried out: "God bless you, sir! O, God bless you, and may you be a Catholic before you die!"

Who can tell how much this poor, friendless woman's prayer had to do with Father Haskins' conversion? In God's sight it weighed more than the supplications of kings. In October, 1830, Rev. Mr. Haskins dissolved his connection with the House of Industry, and accepted a call as rector, in Grace Church, Boston. On December 9, of the same year he was ordained by Bishop Griswold. It is related that while rector of Grace Church, Rev. Mr. Haskins, who always had a leaning towards children, attempted to draw around him the little Irish boys of the North End, by bringing them into his own house, treating them to candy, etc., amusing them with various games, and trying to give them bible lessons. He used to say that the game worked well enough in winter, but, as soon as the fine weather came the birds flew away; when the boys were asked why they didn't come to him, they would answer: "He is only a —— Protestant Minister, why should we listen to him?"

In October, 1830, he resigned his position in Grace Church, Boston, and accepted an engagement in Grace Church, Providence, R. I. Here his labors in the Protestant ministry were crowned with unusual success, though under this outward calm there was a worrying current of doubt and perplexity, which was not lessened by the following incident, related by himself, in a letter, to Father Wiley, some years after.

"I shall never forget," says he, "an old Catholic woman in Providence, that shut up my mouth one evening. One of her family was a Protestant and a member of my parish. I called to see him as was my custom, and began extolling the Episcopal Church, and exhorting him to frequent the Sacraments, but I had better have been a league off, for in the midst of a most eloquent sentence, when talking of *apostolical* succession, and *the bread of life*, and the *body of our Lord*, etc., an aged woman that I had scarcely observed before, who was sitting on a stool in the chimney corner, lifted up her trembling voice and gave me such a terrible dressing that I wished myself anywhere else. 'What!' said she, 'you talk of Apostolic succession! and where is your succession? Who ordained you and your bishop, and the first bishop of your church? If the Catholic Church, then you have shown yourselves by your rebellion and ingratitude the disgrace of your mother and unworthy of her. If not the Catholic Church, then you are usurpers and impostors, and you deceive and lead astray your flocks, and you will have to answer for their souls. Sacraments! Where are your Sacraments? Where your right to administer them?' etc., etc., etc. I was dumb and could not answer. I stammered out something, however, and retired, and soon after I resigned my charge and retired from the duties of a parish, and though often solicited, never accepted another."

It was during Mr. Haskins' stay in Providence

that, in company with his cousin, Rev. Mr. Foxcroft, he paid his second visit to Father Wiley, then residing in Taunton, Mass., and the earnest and learned conversation of this holy priest sank deep into his heart.

Having declined the pastorate of Grace Church, Mr. Haskins returned to his native city, and was appointed Chaplain to the House of Reformation, which position he retained to 1836. During the next few years he filled several offices of trust in Boston.

An entry in his diary dated January 4, 1837, which reads: "Administered communion for the last time as a Protestant, having resolved to do so no more, till I have settled certain religious scruples," shows that his mind was still unsettled in religious matters, and that the good seed was taking root, and in due time would bear fruit. This year (1837) he was unanimously elected Superintendent of the House of Reformation, and, upon his informing the Directors of his religious opinions, his diary says: "They treated me with the utmost kindness and politeness."

Mr. Haskins surrendered his ministry in the Protestant Church into the hands of Bishop Griswold in January, 1839, and in the following May was re-elected Superintendent of the House of Reformation. Again he referred to his religious opinions, and was answered by a (at that time) well-known member of the Board of Directors: "We don't care if you are a Mohammedan, only don't teach the children to follow you."

The following year he resigned his position, severed all the ties that held him to Protestantism, and went to Father Wiley's at Taunton, where after having made a spiritual retreat he made his abjuration and was received into the Catholic Church November, 1840. He shortly afterwards received his first communion, and was confirmed by Rt. Rev. Bishop Fenwick and left for Europe. He visited Rome and several other cities on the Continent, and finally entered the Seminary of St. Sulpice, in Paris.

While in Rome he became acquainted with and was instrumental in the conversion of James R. Bayley, who entered St. Sulpice with him, and who afterwards became Archbishop of Baltimore, Md., Mr. Haskins was also present in Rome when Rev. Alphonse Ratisbonne — the Jew who was miraculously converted by the Blessed Virgin, and who, after laboring most zealously for the conversion of his own race, has lately gone to his reward — made his first communion. This imposing event is beautifully described in Father Haskins' book of travels, a book which we regret to say is, to-day, almost as rare as it is well-written.

Mr. Haskins remained at St. Sulpice about two years, and was ordained in the early part of 1844. He returned to Boston the same year, and on his arrival was sent to Providence, to relieve his spiritual parent, Father Wiley, whose health was declining, and who soon after went to Europe to recruit his strength. Nothing is more beautiful than the holy and tender friendship which united these two hearts, a friendship which lasted until death. A few of the many edifying letters which passed between these two holy priests, while they were separated by the mighty ocean, are still preserved.

In 1846, Father Haskins was appointed Pastor of St. John's Church on Moon Street. Under his administration, the congregation, which had been in existence but three years, increased with extraordinary rapidity. The fact of his being well-known, even before his conversion, attracted large numbers of non-Catholics to the services every Sunday. Naturally of an energetic temperament, and ardently devoted to the service of God, he was a most important accession to the priesthood of Boston, and the work he accomplished will ever keep his name in affectionate remembrance by the priests and people.

As was stated previously, Father Haskins had a strong liking for children, and specially for the orphaned, destitute, and homeless ones, and as soon as he became a priest he devoted all his energies and the means at his command to the bettering of their condition.

After consulting with his Bishop, who not only approved of his designs, but even urged him to put them in execution, giving the Cathedral for the first collection in aid of the good work, Father Haskins gathered a few boys, and placed them under the care of Mr. and Mrs. Cornelius Murphy, in a small building adjoining the Church on Moon Street.

This was the cradle of the House of the Angel Guardian, the first asylum for Catholic orphan boys in New England.

The institution filled so rapidly, that, in 1853, he was obliged to purchase for it a larger estate; this last becoming too contracted, Father Haskins purchased, in 1858, a piece of land in Roxbury, and erected the present building on Vernon Street, to which he transferred his boys in the fall of 1860.

It was about this time that Father Haskins was called upon to receive the last wishes of, and perform the last rites of the Church for, his reverend friend and spiritual father, Rev. William Wiley, who, having set his affairs in order, calmly ended his holy life in the arms of his spiritual son in Christ, April 29, 1855.

During all these years, the congregation of St. John's (thanks to the energy and vigilance of the pastor) had continued to increase; and the church on Moon Street had become too small to contain those who worshipped there.

In 1862, the New Old North Meeting-house, corner Hanover and Clark Streets, was purchased, and dedicated under the patronage of St. Stephen, November 27, of the same year. The dedication was performed by the present Archbishop of Boston, who was then Vicar-general of the diocese.

To this church was transferred the congregation of St. John's; and here Father Haskins continued to labor, with his usual zeal and activity, until his death in 1872.

He also ministered to the congregation of St. Francis de Sales, who attended the chapel of the House of the Angel Guardian, after the old church on Ruggles Street was burned, until they, by his advice, decided to erect another church. As soon, however, as the first steps in the work were taken, he was relieved by Father Sherwood Healy (1867).

The last years of Father Haskins' laborious life were in great part devoted to the permanent establishment of the Institution he had founded, and the reduction of the great debt which pressed so heavily upon it. This he partly succeeded in doing, having reduced it from sixty thousand dollars to thirty thousand dollars in twelve years.

His most ardent desire was to see the "House" in the hands of a religious community; to effect this, he made a voyage to Europe, and another to Canada, to obtain Brothers; but he only obtained promises, which were not fulfilled until nearly two years after his death.

In 1872 he suffered greatly from dropsy and enlargement of the liver; and, feeling his end approaching, retired to his beloved House of the Angel Guardian, where, after regulating his worldly affairs, and receiving the sacraments of Holy Church, he calmly surrendered his soul to God, Saturday evening, October 5, 1872. Thus ended the life of a great and good man, who, ever

HOUSE OF THE ANGEL GUARDIAN.

modest and unostentatious, had even requested that no sermon should be delivered at his funeral; desiring the prayers, but not the praise, of the people among and for whom he had so arduously labored. However, the crowds that visited his remains as they lay in state in St. Stephen's Church, the numerous clergy who attended the funeral services, and the large *cortege* that followed him to his last resting-place, more than expressed the esteem and veneration in which he was held; and the great charity that he founded will ev r keep his memory fresh in the minds and hearts of the Catholics of Boston.

But it is not so much with the founder of this institution, of whom a great deal is already known, this narrative is concerned, as with the Brothers of Charity who have conducted the institution for the past twenty years. Indeed, one of the objects of this sketch is to correct a false idea existing in the minds of many Catholics of New England, namely, that when the saintly Father Haskins died his work and institution died with him. The truth is, that it is only since his death, that his plans have been carried out to completion.

We read in the biography of Father Haskins, of his trip to Europe to secure a community of Brothers, to take charge of the institution he had founded. But he was refused on account of the great want of subjects, which was sorely felt in all communities at that time. As soon as he learned that there was a congregation of religious in Montreal, who bore the title of Brothers of Charity, he made his way thither, and on the 18th of October, 1865, made an application for a colony of these good Brothers to come to Boston and take charge of The House of The Angel Guardian. Notwithstanding his earnest appeal, he was again refused, and the same excuse was put forward, "scarcity of subjects." It was not until January 27th, 1874, after his death, that a colony of six Brothers came to Boston to continue the good work, of which he had laid the foundation.

On that January morning the costly church of Notre Dame, in Montreal, was resounding with words of burning eloquence from some distinguished preacher, portraying God's love for man; the saintly Bishop of that city was engaged in sublime contemplation; the faithful in its many beautiful churches and chapels, with hands uplifted, adored the Creater of this vast universe, and offered Him the incense of devout and ardent prayer; this was the scene these six good Brothers had left behind them, to labor and endure hardships in a new land, and among a strange people. Might not the most heroic heart have shrunk from such a task without being accused of cowardice? The bravest and greatest men who have at any time forsaken their homes, for some noble cause, have often looked back with tearful eyes when they recalled the cheerful hearth, the cherished friends they had forsaken. No one need wonder, then, if these six noble souls had cast a wistful glance on their dear Canadian home, where they had enjoyed, I might say, the luxuries of religion; but no feeling of sadness or fear of disappointment disturbed their peace of mind—and why? Because they placed their trust entirely in the goodness of God, in him, also, who was appointed to be their guide, to be their father.

They knew full well the ability of Brother Justinian, whom we shall now introduce as the first Superior of the Brothers of Charity in Boston. They had known of the sanctity of this Brother since the day he bade farewell to his dear home, in that quaint old province of Belgium called Limburg. They knew his tried and solid virtue, based on deep and genuine humility; and to his wise guidance they intrusted their future and the work they were called to do.

Brother Justinian was no ordinary man. His name is held in benediction even to this day by many of the clergy and people of New England. He was a tireless worker in the vineyard of his Master, and the obliterating wave of time has never wiped away from the minds of the people the great good he effected during his administration. From out the shadows of the past Brother Justinian's character glows with a most beautiful light. He was a man who had received the benediction of hard work. Incessantly busy in

BROTHER JUSTINIAN.

the laudable cause of the institution he was called to govern, he allowed himself very little time for recreation. His noble soul was like a gigantic tree growing in the midst of a great desert, where the weary and heart-stricken came to find shelter from a cruel and censorious world. His life had in it no notes of discord, but was itself a perfect harmony, awakening sweet melodies that drew all who came in contact with him nearer to God and farther away from sin. His influence was exerted not by words alone, but by the silent force of the example of his most saintly life.

Out of regions other than earth came the great shaping forces of his character, and by powers other than the love of fame did he gain mastery over the hearts of all. The great lesson of his life is the witness it bore to the reality of the Divine Savior — Christ. His ready sympathy brought him not only into pleasant relations, but into community of interest and feeling with every one who came in contact with him. He was the nearest friend to the orphan and friendless boys. They recognized the child-heart beneath his manly frame. The erring one was none the less a creature of his solicitude, and with his lofty standard of purity and righteousness, he brought the wanderer back to the path that leads to God. All seemed to see in him the presence of a divine life.

Years passed on peacefully but not uneventfully. The institution prospered. The year 1878 brought a change to the institution. Brother Justinian, whose work in Boston had won the admiration of his superiors abroad, was now to be promoted to the office of Provincial of the American Province. This, of course, would necessitate his changing his home from that of the Angel Guardian Institution to the mother-house of the Province at Montreal. To this new field of labor, as tiresome as it was novel, Brother Justinian applied himself with his usual ardor.

His love for the House of the Angel Guardian and all its associations was in no way lessened. Notwithstanding his many duties, he never forgot his dear Boston home. He often referred to it with words of affection, and watched with interest its advancement.

Before we go further with our narrative, we will tarry a few moments to hear what remains to be told of the life of dear Brother Justinian. For twelve years he filled the office of Provincial. The many trials the Brothers had undergone to establish themselves on this side of the Atlantic were over. The various houses of the Congregation were now in a flourishing condition, when lo! a cloud darker than any yet that had hovered over the young Province, descended and enveloped its members in feelings of the most poignant grief. God asked the life of Brother Justinian. It required strength and extraordinary courage for the members of the community to look this trial in the face and say: "Thy will, O God, be done." But the patient sufferer, bright and cheerful, willingly uttered these beautiful words of reconciliation, and tranquilly awaited the Master's call.

God seemed to have given him the highest favor he can bestow upon his creatures — a vocation to suffer; through all he bore up courageously and cheerfully. Each day he grew weaker and weaker. It became apparent that the end was nearing. The last sacraments were administered. The Brothers gathered at the bedside and gazed upon him who had been their father and guide through many years of trial and hardship.

The twilight of April 16, 1870, waned into darkness, and yet the saintly sufferer lay there. A rapid waning of strength told the good Brothers that the soul must soon leave its prison house. Finally there was a sigh, a groan, a last look of affection, and the great soul of Brother Justinian was with its God; called "to where beyond these voices there is peace."

His inconsolable brethren bent over that prostrate form and longed to hear once more his voice. But those lips that had so often spoken to them words of encouragement when they were disheartened — lips that had so often pointed out the path of duty — were now hushed forever. The light had gone from their pathway, the music of their home was hushed. If they gave way to the sadness of the hour it was because they were weighed down with a remembrance of those trials through which the young American Province had passed, and of the great fight with discouragement, in which he who had died had led them to victory and healed them of their hurts by his own courage and sight of the peace to come.

Clothed in his humble religious habit, reverently and lovingly the mortal remains of Brother Justinian were placed on a couch draped in white. At his head stood a little stand, on which were a large crucifix and two lighted wax tapers, whose gentle, gleaming light shone on the serene face, now cold in death. For two sad days and nights the Brothers clustered around their beloved Superior, but even this sad privilege soon had to be relinquished. No sound, save the solemn chant of the Brothers, broke the profound stillness of the convent as the mortal remains of Brother Justinian were lovingly and mournfully consigned to their place in the Brothers' vault. There they laid him, far away from his dear old home in distant Belgium, to await the resurrection morn.

CHAPTER V.

Rt. Rev. J. B. Fitzpatrick, First President of Trustees of the House of The Angel Guardian — Most Rev. J. J. Williams, Second President — Rev. M. P. Dougherty, First Secretary of the House of the Angel Guardian.

John Bernard Fitzpatrick was born at Boston, November 1, 1812. The education of John Bernard was commenced at home, under the instruction of his honest and virtuous parents. That home was not only a school for the mind, but it was also a temple for the soul, where good parental example and early religious inculcation made a lasting impression upon the young members of that happy household. The first lessons in secular learning that he received outside of his own family were imparted in the primary and

Rt. Rev. Bishop Fitzpatrick.

grammar schools of Boston, in which he greatly distinguished himself, and gave proofs of his future eminence. He received the Franklin medals as the reward of his assiduity and good conduct. In 1826 he entered the Boston Latin School, from which he graduated with the highest honors, leaving after him the reputation of a model student, a favorite companion, and an exemplar of Christian youth. Between his teachers and young Fitzpatrick was maintained a lifelong friendship. In the midst of elements most hostile to his faith and Church, he clung to these with unwavering fidelity and love. The eye of the venerable Bishop Fenwick soon perceived the treasure which the Church possessed in young Fitzpatrick, whose noble bearing and solid virtues attracted his attention, gained his confidence, and won his affection. Under the advice and patronage of the bishop, he took leave of his family and friends, and, at the age of seventeen, entered Montreal College, in September, 1829. Here he made a thorough course of classical studies, with honor and distinction. His deportment was edifying, and his life pure; his piety and love of virtue became the admiration of all. In 1837, having finished his course at Montreal, his superiors determined to send him to the Seminary of St. Sulpice, at Paris, the nursery of profound learning and exalted virtues. Here in the midst of two hundred students, the flower of France and of Europe, the American levite soon became conspicuous, and in less than a year was regarded as the ornament of the seminary. The venerable superior of the Sulpitians then predicted that young Fitzpatrick would one day rise to high position in the Church, and become an ornament to its hierarchy. His studies completed, he was now ripe for the holy calling which had been the great object of his life, studies, prayers, and discipline. He was accordingly promoted to the holy priesthood June 13, 1840, at the age of twenty-seven. In November, 1840, he returned to Boston, the chosen field of his labors. His first mission was at the Cathedral. Here he devoted himself to hearing confessions; instructing children, the poor, and the ignorant in their religious duties; and in visiting the sick. After a year thus engaged, he was appointed pastor of East Cambridge. Here he soon raised a substantial stone church, in which his fervid eloquence and truly priestly life and labors accomplished much good. In 1844, the declining health of Bishop Fenwick, and the ever increasing labors of his arduous office, rendered it impossible for him to postpone longer the appointment of a coadjutor to assist him in his administration. The bishop's wishes were concurred in, and the priest of his choice was given him as his coadjutor and successor. He was consecrated at Georgetown, on Sunday, March 4, 1844, by Bishop Fenwick. On entering upon his new career, he commenced by prescribing rigid rules for his own conduct and management of affairs, which he carefully observed, and which guided him with remarkable safety and success through the many spiritual and temporal cares of his journey. He immediately took up his residence at the episcopal mansion in Franklin Street, and the old Cathedral became the field of his zealous toil. His sermons were very impressive, eloquent, and convincing; and were attended by a great number of Protestants, many of whom became converted to the faith.

In 1846 the venerable Bishop Fenwick died; and thenceforth the whole responsibility of this diocese, embracing all New England, Rhode Island and Connecticut excepted, devolved upon Bishop Fitzpatrick. The cross which he embraced now bore heavily upon his shoulders, with no one to share it but Him who bore it for us all. During years of single-handed labor, his heart was on many occasions afflicted. It was his lot in 1854 to witness the blowing up of a church in course of erection at Dorchester by some unknown ruffians, and, in the same year, the burning of the church in Bath, the Knownothing riot in Manchester, N. H., and the Ellsworth outrage.

The most practical test of his labors and their results may be found in these simple facts: from two dioceses there are now seven; from forty priests and as many churches in 1844, there were at the time of his death three hundred priests and three hundred churches, more than one hundred of each being in the diocese of Boston alone. Though comparatively young when first attacked by the disease which finally caused his death, and frequently warned of the constant danger he was in, he continued his personal labors and exertions with unabated energy. He was frequently advised by his friends and colleagues to relax his application to work; but, as long as he was capable of laboring, he never allowed himself rest. He discovered his error, alas! too late. His health grew daily more and more precarious. For many years before his death he was an invalid and a great sufferer. In his solicitude for his flock, and in his desire to provide a father for them in case of his death, he gave his attention to the important matter of selecting his successor. He fixed his choice upon the present distinguished prelate who occupies the archiepiscopal see of Boston. During his eight years of pain and anguish, his people, who had so much admired him in health, now honored and venerated more than ever the patient sufferer. As an evidence of his generous thoughtfulness for others, as well as his love for the land of his fathers, it is related of him, that while he was an exile from his diocese, in Europe, where he had gone in search of health a few years before his death, the famine broke out in Ireland; his tender heart was melted at the sufferings of that woe-stricken people. "The wail of suffering reached his ear;" and immediately from his sick-bed he wrote to Boston a letter of affectionate entreaty, imploring his people to hasten to the relief of the famishing sons of St. Patrick. A beautiful trait of the bishop's character was a love of truth. His very countenance, his general bearing, his conversation, all testified to the truth within him. The hypocrite and dissembler trembled in his presence, and dared not look him in the face. For the contrite wrong-doer he was full of compassion and forgiveness, but the deceiver he would never brook. His displeasure extended even to those who, to entertain company, invented stories or exaggerated facts; and he usually manifested it by refusing to join in the laugh or by adroitly changing the current of conversation. There was no obscurity in his language or writings, because there was no duplicity in his heart. Strong faith and decision of character were prominent traits in the Bishop's character. His long illness and protracted sufferings only served to bring out with greater lustre his many exalted traits. His death was worthy of his life,— calm, resigned, devout, and noble to the last. On the Saturday before he died, raising high the hand that held the crucifix, he said: "The dark veil will soon be drawn from my eyes, as the gloomy winter passes before the spring; I will follow the cross to the end."

Bishop Fitzpatrick expired Tuesday, February 13, 1866, in the fifty-fourth year of his age; and the Church mourned one of her most illustrious prelates, whose memory is in benediction.

Most Rev. J. J. Williams.

For the greater part of the present inhabitants of Boston, Theatre Alley, once so famous, is only a memory, a thing of the past. To the Catholics of Boston it should be hallowed ground; for here was born, April 27, 1822, the present Archbishop of Boston, J. J. Williams.

At the age of four years he was placed at school, under the charge of Mrs. Newmarch. After two years, he was transferred to the school in the basement of the old Cathedral on Franklin Street, under the control of Rev. James Fitton. Though not distinguished by his talents, his early life at school manifested the dispositions, which grew with the man, and formed part of his being. Application and love of truth, hatred of sham, and self-sacrifice, were traits of his character from his earliest years, and make him to-day the beau-ideal prelate of America.

While at this school he seemed to manifest a vocation for the sanctuary, and at the age of eleven he was sent to Montreal College, Canada, then, as now, under the charge of the Society of

Most Rev. John J. Williams, D.D.

St. Sulpice. Here he remained eight years, a close student, beloved by all, teachers and students. In 1841 he went to France, and entered the Seminary of St. Sulpice, at Paris. Here in the capital of the world, in all that relates to art and science, he spent four years, a keen observer of men and events. Before his return to Boston, in 1845, he was ordained by Archbishop Affre, and assigned to the Cathedral, the Sunday school being placed under his special care. In 1855 he was made rector of the Cathedral, and a few years later Vicar-general of the diocese.

During the long years of sickness that preceded the death of Bishop Fitzpatrick, Vicar-general Williams administered the affairs of the diocese with prudence and judgment. In matters of dispute, all looked to him, as certain to decide with fairness, and according to strict justice. Even the most intimate friends could not bias or warp his opinions. Favoritism, the curse of so many well-meaning men in power, has never been laid to his charge; and, after twenty-seven years, it may be said of him, with truth, that he has never willingly wronged any one in his episcopal administration.

At the time of his consecration, the diocese of Boston included all the State of Massachusetts. Since then, the diocese of Springfield (including the counties of Berkshire, Franklin, Hampshire, Hampden, and Worcester), and the diocese of Providence (including Bristol, Barnstable, and part of Plymouth counties), were created.

To-day the Archdiocese of Boston has 170 churches, 376 priests, and 30,000 children in the parochial schools. The churches throughout the diocese are, for the most part, objects of pride to the Catholic heart, because of their beauty and elegance. After years of patient struggle, their financial condition is such as to warrant the belief that before many years have passed they will be entirely relieved of the monster debt. Schools are multiplying every year. The sick, the orphan, and the outcast are provided for. While last, but not least, the new seminary at Brighton has already entered on its career of usefulness in preparing candidates for the work of ministry.

This work has been for years the subject of the Archbishop's thoughts. Not a detail of its construction has escaped his notice; and it stands to-day a monument to the zeal and piety of the clergy of Boston, their tribute of love and affection to their well-beloved Archbishop. In the building of the Cathedral, he received valuable aid from the late Vicar-general P. F. Lyndon; but the seminary is his own work, to which he has given his heart and brain. May he live to see his plans realized, and to know that he has established here, in his diocese, a system of ecclesiastical training and education second to none in the world! And, when God calls him to receive his reward, may he depart this life with the consciousness that the tribunals of Rome have never been called upon to adjucate in any controversy or trial between him and his priests!

Rev. Manasses P. Dougherty.

The Rev. Manasses P. Dougherty, who died pastor of St. Peter's Church, Cambridge, was one of the typical priests of New England, having been linked in ecclesiastical career with what may be termed the missionary days of the diocese, and having lived to witness the great development of Catholicity here, in which he was a zealous factor.

He was born in Ireland, in 1816, and came to America at an early age. On August 28, 1842, he was ordained at the Sulpician Seminary, Montreal, and having remained at that Institution until November 6th, same year, he began his priestly labors under Bishop Fenwick in the diocese of Boston. He was at once appointed to take charge of the mission at Benedicta Plantation, Aroostook County, Maine. The autograph copy of the letter from the Bishop giving him his commission, which bears date November 7, 1842, is still preserved, and is an interesting souvenir. It opens by saying: "Your mission embraces the towns of Benedicta and Houlton and the country within

REV. FATHER DOUGHERTY.

the limits of the United States adjacent to them. Your residence will be in Benedicta; Houlton you will visit occasionally." The letter proceeds to give special instructions on the importance of counteracting intemperance by the promotion of temperance societies, and of catechizing the young.

It appears that to make marriages legal, according to Maine laws, it was required that a clergyman should receive, at the discretion of the Governor, a State Commission; and accordingly, Father Dougherty received from Governor Fairfield the necessary document, dated January 2, 1843, in which he is referred to as worthy of "special trust and confidence, for sobriety, discretion, and piety."

In May, 1844, after preparing for the foundation of churches at Houlton and Benedicta, he was transferred to St. John's Church, East Cambridge, Mass., and through his earnest efforts St. Peter's Church, Cambridge, was erected in 1848, Father Dougherty becoming the successor to Bishop Fitzpatrick on his elevation to the

Episcopate. The corner-stone of St. Peter's was laid by Bishop Fitzpatrick, on the 12th of July, 1848. Divine service was conducted in the church the following year by Father Dougherty, who held its pastorate up to the time of his death. In the first year he baptized one hundred and thirty-five persons at St. Peter's. Being wholly occupied with the interests of this parish, he relinquished St. John's. He left to his successors as one of the results of his efforts a commodious pastoral residence. Previous to the date of his building St. Peter's, his parish included old Cambridge, Cambridgeport, Somerville, Medford, Malden, West Cambridge, and Lexington. He celebrated Mass once a fortnight in Medford, and once a week in Lexington. All the others attended Cambridge. In time there were churches built in Lexington and Medford.

In the fall of 1859 Father Dougherty's health being poor, his pastoral charge was for a time supplied by Rev. George F. Haskins, the beloved founder of the House of the Angel Guardian. On a certain evening during his illness, Father

Haskins called to see him, and presented him with a note, saying: "The sexton of your church gave me this note for you this morning." Father Dougherty opened it, and to his astonishment found a thousand dollars sent to him as a present from the congregation of St. Peter's. He was advised by his physician to take a season of rest abroad, and on the 25th of July, 1860, he received a letter from Bishop Fitzpatrick instructing him to do so. On the following Sunday he announced to the congregation his purpose to visit Ireland. As an evidence of his popularity, it may be mentioned that the sum of five hundred dollars was promptly raised by seventeen young men of the parish, and a felicitous address was presented with it. On arrival in his native land, he received new greetings from clergy and laity, and was presented with an address of welcome to the parish of Donagh, signed by the pastor and prominent laymen.

The increase of the Catholics of Cambridge made it necessary to have another church, and Father Dougherty took the necessary steps for the erection of St. Mary's Church, Cambridgeport, the corner-stone of which was laid July 15, 1866. He continued the work until May, 1867, when the completion was undertaken by the present pastor, the Rev. Thomas Scully, the church being opened in 1868. In 1874 Father Dougherty organized a new parish in Cambridge under the name of St. Paul's, purchasing the church of the Congregational Society on the corner of Mount Auburn and Holyoke Streets.

He retained the pastorate of St. Paul's in addition to St. Peter's until October 1, 1874, when he was succeeded by the Rev. William Orr. In addition to the above he built the fine church which adorns the town of Arlington.

Father Dougherty's work was everywhere characterized by zeal and devotion. He was generous and hospitable in a rare degree, and many who needed his aid will long remember the cheerful readiness with which he tendered it. On one occasion he gave a check for $1000 to the President of Boston College, enjoining at the same time strict secrecy as to the donor. He was one of the first incorporators of the House of the Angel Guardian, and up to the time of his death was Secretary of the Board of Trustees. In all the trials and difficulties attendant upon the foundation and government of so large an institution, Father Haskins had no truer friend nor wiser counsellor than Father Dougherty. To him the founder confided his cares and hopes, and from him never failed to receive the encouragement he needed. As an illustration of the prominent and esteemed position in which he was held in the estimation of the clergy, it may be stated that on various occasions when testimonials were presented to the Bishop of the diocese on their behalf, he was always given a prominent part in representing them.

His death took place July 25, 1877, in the sixty-first year of his age, and his funeral services, which occurred on the 27th, were attended by a remarkably large concourse of clergy and laity. An eloquent tribute to the beloved pastor was delivered by the Rev. Robert Fulton, S. J. In June, 1878, the Catholics of Cambridge gave evidence of their remembrance by the erection of a beautiful monument over his grave. Inscribed upon it are the words: "This monument was erected by the parishioners of St. Peter's Church in grateful remembrance of his long and devoted service as pastor in the vineyard of the Lord. Requiescat in Pace."

BROTHER HILDUWARD,

CHAPTER VI.

ELECTION OF BROTHER HILDUWARD TO THE OFFICE OF PROVINCIAL — CONTINUATION OF THE HISTORY OF THE HOUSE OF THE ANGEL GUARDIAN — ELECTION OF BROTHER WENCESLAUS — HE IS TRANSFERRED TO WATERFORD, IRELAND — ELECTION OF BROTHER EUSEBIUS — DEATH OF BROTHER EUSEBIUS.

The human heart having once dwelt on the long sought heights of peacefulness and happiness, and being held there by the very fascination of the moment, feels a pang when the drift of circumstances forces it to descend and take with the same accustomed grace, the ordinary tasks of life. Methinks there are few of us strong enough to visit the chamber of some loved one who has been swept away by the merciless hand of death, without feeling emotions of inexpressible sadness. But these were the emotions the good Brothers had to meet and suppress after the death of their beloved Superior. It was quite impossible for them at this moment to realize that his great fatherly presence was to be seen in their convent home no more; that Brother Justinian was no longer in the world. With saddened hearts they began anew their various duties. They must try to forget their trouble and be reconciled to the will of Heaven. After a short respite the chapter assembled, and to the joy of all, the American Province had again a guide in the person of Brother Hilduward.

Brother Hilduward is in every sense of the word a gentleman of the French type. Those who know him best love him most. His years of varied experience in all the works embraced by the Congregation, combined with sound common sense and administrative ability, make him equal to the task imposed upon him. His position calls for powers of administration of the highest order; and whilst his services are demanded by the Brothers in every difficulty, he administers the details of his position in a most efficient way.

BROTHER WENCESLAUS.

Brother Hilduward has within him keen intelligence, bound up with a spiritual power that makes him "the right man in the right place." May he live long to guide the destiny of the American Province is the fervent wish and prayer of the writer.

Having digressed from our narrative, we will now return to the Angel Guardian Home, and trace its history from the day Brother Justinian was elected Provincial to the present time. We said before that this new office obliged him to make his home at the Mother House in Montreal. A Superior had to be elected for the House of the Angel Guardian.

Brother Wenceslaus was chosen to fill the vacant place. He took up the work just where Brother Justinian had left it. After filling the position for three years he was called by his Superior to govern a new institution at Waterford, Ireland. During his administration at the House of the Angel Guardian, steady growth and success crowned the institution.

Brother Eusebius, formerly the Provincial of the

American Province, was elected as successor to Brother Wenceslaus at the House of the Angel Guardian. The following notice of his sudden death, as chronicled in one of the local papers of Montreal, shows the great worth of the man, and the esteem in which he was held by all classes:

A Laborious Career Closed. Death of Brother Eusebius, of Montreal.

A long life, eminent for its usefulness in the service of the poor and the afflicted, terminated in Montreal, July 28th, with the death of Brother Eusebius, Superior of the Brothers of Charity in charge of the St. Benoit-Joseph Asylum at Longue Pointe, P. Q. Recovering from an indisposition which had seized him while returning from a trip to St. Ferdinand, Halifax, on the 25th, he had made preparations for a voyage to Europe by the next steamboat. On the morning assigned for his departure it was noticed that he did not appear as early as usual, and a Brother was sent to his room to ascertain if he needed anything. No

BROTHER EUSEBIUS.

answer having been returned to his knock, the Brother entered and found Brother Eusebius dressed, having risen from bed to add another day to the long bead-string of his unselfish life, but seated in a chair, with his head a little inclined to one side, as if sleeping. The messenger noiselessly retired, and returning to those who had sent him, reported that Brother Eusebius was sleeping in his chair. This was deemed improbable, and he was sent back to make a closer observation. It was then discovered that the tireless laborer was truly sleeping, but it was the sleep that knows no waking.

The deceased Brother's name in the world was Eusebe de Poorter. He was born in Ypres, Belgium, March 17, 1817, of noble parentage. On March 27, 1842, he entered the Brotherhood of Charity, making his profession August 14, 1843. Within a comparatively brief space of time he was appointed successively Superior of Houses in Louvain, Bruges, and Ghent. He received an equal vote with another member of the Congregation for the office of Superior-General in 1862.

Accompanied by Brothers Sebastian, Edmond, and Linus, he came to Canada in 1865, establishing the first mission of his order in St. Anthony's Asylum, Montreal. In 1873 the Canadian government found that they could not do better than to give the custody of the Montreal reformatory for juvenile delinquents, now the model institution of its class in North America, to Brother Eusebius and his brethren. It was from here that, in 1874, by the invitation of the Most Rev. Archbishop Williams, he sent a number of Brothers to take charge of the House of the Angel Guardian. He returned to his native land in 1880, where, for two years, he was assistant Superior in one of the Parent Houses; after which he came to Boston and earned the esteem of clergy and laity by his admirable management of the House of the Angel Guardian. Fresh pioneer work was found for him in 1884, at St. Anthony's Orphan Asylum, Detroit, Michigan, where he, with six other members of the order, succeeded the Franciscan Brothers. Having established the affairs of this institution upon a firm basis, he was finally assigned

to the Brothers' great asylum for epileptics and the insane, at Longue Pointe, P. Q., which he directed until his death.

The place in the Lord's vineyard left vacant by the decease of Brother Eusebius will not easily be filled. His loss will be felt by the entire Province of Quebec, which was the field of the greater part of his labors. The Reformatory of Montreal, which may be said to have been created by Brother Eusebius, is a blessing by which all Canada has been benefited. Loved and esteemed by those confided to his guidance, he had the unlimited confidence of his superiors, who relied on him for the performance of work demanding tact, business knowledge, and special powers of administrative ability. The sudden termination of his life was the result of heart disease, and was in accordance with his expectation for years. It found him prepared, both spiritually and temporally. On July 30, after a Solemn Requiem High Mass in the Montreal Reformatory, attended by a large number of priests and other friends, his remains were borne to the crypt beneath, and finally laid to rest.

Brother Joseph was the next into whose hands the reins of government fell. On April 24, 1884, he entered into his new office. He was a man filled with the spirit of his vocation, and was beloved by all who knew him. He filled the office of Superior for five years, and was then called to the reward of his labors by the Divine Master, in whose vineyard he labored so long and zealously. The following account of his death appeared in the "Orphans' Friend" of that year:

Death of Brother Joseph.

"In the midst of life we are in death." The full significance of these words was realized by every inmate of the House of the Angel Guardian on the 8th of September last. In the morning Brother Joseph attended Mass in the chapel, receiving holy communion as usual. Subsequently he breakfasted with the community, and was afterwards met in various parts of the House. At dinner he was

BROTHER JOSEPH.

missed from the table, and a Brother was sent to the infirmary to inquire if he desired to have the meal served there. Words fail to convey an idea of the shock received by Brother Jude and the other members of the community when the messenger announced that Brother Joseph was dead.

For years previously Brother Joseph's life was that of a martyr. He suffered untold agony from an incurable abscess; yet, until within a few months back, he went about performing his full duties with a smiling countenance, and without complaint. At length, in June last, he was obliged to place himself under treatment in Carney Hospital, whence, after a stay of four weeks, he returned much improved, but under orders to refrain from all active occupation. Except for this affliction, greatly aggravated by a hereditary corpulence, he was a healthy man, so that his death, caused by the rupture of a blood-vessel, was unexpected by all who knew him.

Brother Joseph, whose baptismal name was Onezime Hamel, was born in Quebec, March 29, 1844, and became a Brother of Charity October

27, 1866. On April 24, 1884, he succeeded Brother Eusebius as Superior of the community in the House of the Angel Guardian, in which office, by his unfailing courtesy and zeal for the mission of the Institution, he won the esteem of all with whom he had relations. His chief work in the House was its enlargement two years ago by the addition of a new wing. But a better memorial of his beneficent life, is the love of the hundreds of boys who now mourn his loss. The body, in care of Provincial Justinian, was conveyed to Montreal, and was interred in the cemetery of the Congregation, September 11th. May he rest in peace!

The following account of the Industrial School was published in a Boston journal dated June the 4th, 1891. It will give the reader an idea of the beginning of the great work:

THE INDUSTRIAL SCHOOL OF THE HOUSE OF
THE ANGEL GUARDIAN.

At last the trade school of the House of The Angel Guardian is finished. It was practically

Composing Room—Angel Guardian Industrial School.

completed May 20, when the trade departments, already in operation, began to move into it. Its exterior, as viewed from Ruggles Street, on which it fronts, or from Westminster Street, which terminates right opposite, is not imposing. It is not a "palace of industry;" but it is neat, while being modest.

Within there is ample space for all the purposes at present contemplated. As stated in previous accounts, the basement, with cemented floor, is occupied by the bakery and press room. The pressman, Brother Peter, and his assistants, rejoice with feelings too intense for expression at their removal from the temporary quarters. Three presses are in operation; one for newspaper and book-work, and two for job printing. There is also a 30-inch paper cutter. All are driven by an Edison electric motor of 3-horse power, supplied by the Suburban Electric Light Company, with a current of 5000 volts. The oven and other apparatus of the bakery are constructed on the most improved models.

On the next floor, right above the press room,

is the composing room, supplied abundantly with shelves and closets. An office for the proof-reader, enclosed by partitions half of ornamental wire-work and half of varnished wood, occupies one corner. Opposite is the business office, occupying a small ell attached to the front of the building. In the main room are compositors' stands and cases for a dozen or more type-setters, arranged beside the broad rear windows; a job cabinet, three imposing stones, proof press, galley and lead racks, card and lead cutters, and other printers' tools too numerous to mention. The work comprises job, newspaper, and book printing.

On the other side of the main entry, but upon the same floor, is the shoe shop, of rather limited dimensions at present, but adequate for all needs as far as they can be now foreseen, besides offices for the Brother superintending and the door-keeper.

The tailors are airily located in a commodious room on the top floor, immediately above the shoe shop. The rest of the floor is designed to serve

Folding and Delivery Room—Angel Guardian Industrial School.

as a reading room for the working boys, but for the present it will be used for storage.

All the shops are under the direct supervision of the Brothers, one or more of whom is always in attendance; but the instructors in the various trades are laymen.

So far, the printing office is the most developed of all departments. Ten boys are working at the cases, three or four showing marked progress for the short time they have been learning the trade; while three lads are employed in the press room, two of whom are already experts in running the job presses, and are accomplished feeders for the cylinder press. Besides "The Orphan's Friend" and "The Bouquet," both of which speak for themselves, some good work has been put out by the office in the form of business cards, hand-bills, bill-heads, advertising programmes, and society lists.

Very little less is the progress shown by the tailors. Two classes are made in this trade. The first one, whose chief work is repairing, and in which general sewing is taught, remains in the old quarters in the main building. The new shop is devoted entirely to the advanced class, comprising ten boys, each able to sew satisfactorily an entire suit of clothes, and now receiving instruction in fitting and cutting.

Shoemaking comes next in the order of progress. In this department is done all the repairing needed by the institution. Hand-sewed and machine-sewed shoes of the best finish are likewise made here. So far, however, the orders are not sufficient to occupy more than two boys beside the foreman. It is, however, expected that there will soon be a sufficiency of work to employ ten or a dozen boys in this department.

This trade school supplies a want long felt by the institution. The best efforts of its directors to give the orphan boys committed to their charge a fair start in life have often failed because of the boys' inability to help themselves. After this, lads who have completed the two years' course of instruction in this school, however friendless they may be, when leaving the institution will carry with them a knowledge which will always

Press Room—Angel Guardian Industrial School.

enable them to make an honest livelihood. It is not too much to say that thereby the usefulness of the House will be increased four-fold.

The work should enlist the sympathy and aid, not only of the Catholic community, but of all lovers of humanity or social order. It is a charity of the highest benevolence, and it offers a channel for the performance of a duty dictated by every feeling of our nature, as by our wisest sense of self-interest. In the words of Brother Jude, to erect this school, "the first cent was borrowed," increasing the debt on the institution to $30,000; but few will say that in this case the end did not justify the means. The expense cannot fail to prove a trifle compared to the advantages secured to the community, and it is confidently anticipated that the generosity which has heretofore maintained the institution, will need no further stimulus than the work itself to make it a complete and creditable success.

———

Since the publication of this article the Industrial School has been enlarged and improved to such an extent that this description does no longer give it a true portrayal. In the press room there are now nine presses, which keep a number of boys constantly employed. In the composing room twenty boys are kept busily at work. The other departments have undergone similar improvements.

Admirable Work of the Brothers of Charity.

As the problem of managing and training wayward boys, or those that become a care upon the public, is a perplexity to our civil authorities, it may be of interest to note a visit to an institution in Canada, where the diverse difficulties are overcome. It is the Reform School of the Brothers of Charity of Montreal, in which the Government of the Province of Quebec has placed wayward boys for training and reformation, as sentenced by the courts.

The visitor is surprised from the first entrance with the sense of order and quiet which prevails, and soon finds that here he is in the presence of

Juvenile Band of the Brothers' House at Montreal.

discipline that is effectual without rigor, and firm without harshness. Here are hundreds of boys from the smallest to the largest, most of whom were committed to the Brothers because unmanageable either by parental or local authority, and yet all in ready and apparently cheerful submission to the rules and work; all appropriately classified according to age, disposition, training, and other conditions. The smaller boys are busily engrossed with their studies in the school rooms, and the larger ones are occupied at certain hours in learning and practising various trades, including carpentry, shoemaking, carriage making, blacksmithing, and painting. That this work is genuine and productive, is evidenced by the bulk and value of its results, which are in active demand among traders throughout the Province, owing to the thoroughness and durability of workmanship. Each of the rooms is occupied by one or more of the Brothers of Charity, whose presence without any apparent effort, commands respectful attention and quiet. This is not by any means a prison, though embracing so many who should have been committed to prison but for its beneficent influence, and the entire stress of the restraining and reforming work is based upon religious means. The arrangements for the cleanliness, decency, and healthful condition of the inmates are manifest, especially in the dormitories, bath, and dining rooms for the boys. Everything is conducted with a rigid regard for decorum, and the attention of the Brothers in these particulars illustrates the saying that "eternal vigilance is the price of freedom." It is in the chapel that the highest moral effect of the Brothers' influence is felt; and when the devoted members of the Society are congregated on a Sunday, with all the inmates of the adopted family, and hundreds of fresh and resonant voices are chanting hymns in unison, one can well imagine himself in the midst of a strictly religious community. Probably nowhere on this continent is religion more zealously enlisted in the work of saving and training boys than under the Brothers of Charity, and nowhere are its fruits more pleasing and salutary.

BROTHER JUDE.

PRESENT SUPERIOR OF THE HOUSE OF THE ANGEL GUARDIAN.

CHAPTER VII.

Election of Brother Jude, Present Superior — The Rapid Advancement of the House of The Angel Guardian — The Amount of Good Being Done in the Cause of Orphanage.

Those who have followed us thus far in our narrative, will no doubt have some faint idea of the House of The Angel Guardian and its work. It will be noticed that each of the Superiors of the Institution did his share to bring about the grand results we enjoy to-day. But the Institution nor its works never reached the fulness of completion until the Chapter elected Brother Jude, the present Superior, as successor to Brother Joseph. From the very day he was commanded by his Superior to take upon himself this grave responsibility, he has been the pivot upon which the affairs of the growing Institution have turned. Among the Superiors of the House of The Angel Guardian his name must stand pre-eminent. He has the attributes of mind that peculiarly fit him for leadership—purity of intention and indomitable will. Straightforward in purpose, never vacillating, he has a clear understanding of duty, and performs it most faithfully. He has shown from the beginning a wonderful talent for administration. But it is not on this account that the hearts of the many friends of the Institution go out to him in love and reverence. It is rather because there is seen in his every word and act purity of intention and love of God. It is impossible to estimate the good he has accomplished during his administration.

An Industrial School for the boys was the first great work he undertook. He had the project long in mind, but as the necessary means were not forthcoming, he started out with the little he had at hand, and established a printing department in a small building that had been used as a stable. With the printing department he estab-

Ga--- and Yard—House of the Angel Guardian.

lished a small eight page weekly, titled "The Orphan's Bouquet." To carry on the work successfully it was evident that a more commodious building was necessary, and venturing still further, the good Brother, trusting upon Divine Providence, laid the foundation of a new building on Ruggles Street, which was completed May 20, 1891. To this the printing department was removed, and a tailor's shop and bakery were added.

This involved the Superior in a debt of several thousand dollars. The prospects were rather dark and the financial emergencies pressing, when suddenly the little weekly journal took a start and made its way through the entire country. Its list of subscribers swelled high, and in one year the paper was increased from eight to sixteen pages, and, later on, to twenty pages, the subscription list swelling to ten thousand. The journal can now take its place among the best literary publications in the land. It has become an ideal family story paper, and has among its contributors some of the ablest Catholic writers of the day. Bishops and clergy have given it their warmest support and sanction. Thus has God watched over the progress of the work of Brother Jude; and its almost miraculous advancement shows beyond a doubt that the protecting hand of Divine Providence is guiding it on to accomplish greater things.

Nowhere is Brother Jude more highly esteemed and loved than in the Institution over which he presides. He is the sunshine of the home; a power in a place where his penetrating eye can see what is needful to mold the characters of those boys placed under his charge, who have reached a time of life when their minds are impressionable and easily turned one way or the other.

It is a source of great gratification to those connected with the Institution that the health of the good Superior remains so well, notwithstanding the many cares and anxieties that tax his strength. While he is at the helm to guide the work of the House of The Angel Guardian we can expect to see wonderful things accomplished in the way of alleviating misery and distress.

INFIRMARY—HOUSE OF THE ANGEL GUARDIAN.

The love uniting the Brothers and boys of the Institution to Brother Jude is strikingly manifested in the following account of one of his feast-day celebrations. It shows their respect for authority, and their deep love for their beloved Superior:

THE ORPHANS' TRIBUTE TO BROTHER JUDE ON HIS PATRONAL FEAST.

BY T. A. DWYER, A. B.

Namesake of him whose zeal for Christ,
 And scorn of all this world's renown,
In God's own chosen time, sufficed
 To merit him a martyr's crown.

Behold! once more the circling year
 Brings back thy blessed Patron's feast,
And finds thy children gathered here
 With filial love for thee increased.

And strange it were, in sooth, if love
 For thee we lacked, dear Brother Jude,
Whose lot it has been long to prove
 Thy vigilant solicitude.

Here shielded from all want and woe,
 And trained alike in mind and heart,
To thee and to thy care we owe
 The blessings whereof we have part.

What shall we wish thee, then, to-day?
 Ah! if our wishes, Brother Jude,
Could bring thee all our hearts would say,
 Thou had'st of joys a plenitude.

Long years of blissful days be thine
 And strength to do the Master's will,
And when thy faithful hands resign
 The work they now so well fulfil—

May the great glory that he won
 The name which now is thine who bore,
When thy life's labors here are done,
 Reward thy toil forevermore.

We present here a letter written by a prominent lawyer in Boston, which testifies to the real, earnest, Christian work the House of the Angel Guardian is constantly doing.

Dear Brother Jude:—

In reference to the boy I spoke to you about last night, I beg to say that to-day the matter came up for disposition, and the Court finally consented to impose a fine on him of six dollars. This very lenient action of the magistrate of course obviated the necessity of my asking you to add the responsibility of him to your already burdened shoulders.

The cheerfulness you manifested in consenting to take him, if by the Court you were allowed so

INTERIOR OF THE CHAPEL—HOUSE OF THE ANGEL GUARDIAN.

to do, impels me to ask you, in behalf of the boy you so willingly consented to aid, *free of charge*, to accept my warmest and most grateful acknowledgements. I sincerely trust the public may know more of the grand work being done by your Institution, for I must admit that facts I learned by a personal visit to the Home have opened my eyes.

If I can be of service any time do not hesitate to call on me.

Wishing you God speed, I remain,

Very sincerely yours,

It would be impossible to enumerate here the number of boys that have been saved from a life of recklessness and sin by being harbored in the Institution. We rejoice to believe that there is still greater work for the Institution to do in the future than it has ever done in the past.

> There are orphans by the score
> In the village and the city;
> Indigence knocks at our door,
> Hunger cries to us for pity;
> And the sobs of pain and dearth
> Sadden half the songs of earth.

As long as suffering, disappointment, effort, sorrow, and death shall exist in this world, the affliction belonging to them shall also exist. The poor will be always with us. The following beautiful verses, published in "The Orphan's Bouquet" of October 1, 1891, clearly illustrate the great lesson the House of The Angel Guardian is teaching to the world:

>Not so great a truth He told
> As a mandate He appointed,
>Who, in Bethany of old,
> Was by Mary's hands anointed,
>When He said, "While days endure
>You will always have the poor."
>
>Since the hour to Bethlehem,
> When His parents went together,
>And no dwelling sheltered them,
> Save a stable from the weather,
>There has been nor time nor spot
>That the poor were with us not.
>
>Agar, homeless in the East,
> Ruth, the gleaner in the meadows,
>Lazarus, at Dives' feast,
> Crouching in the outer shadows;
>And the beggar at the gates,
>All are types time iterates.
>
>And whenever Want may plead,

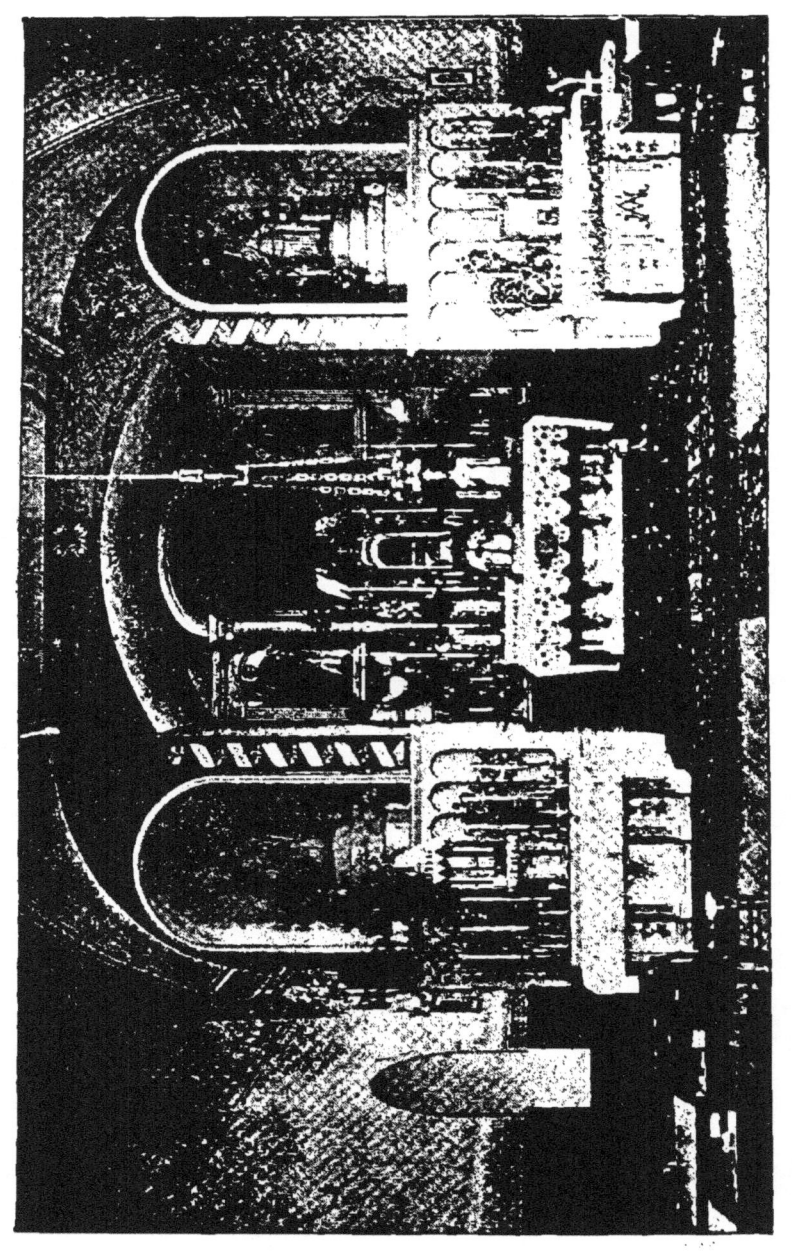

The Altars in Chapel of the House of the Angel Guardian.

In whatever form or fashion,
They its voice who fail to heed,
  Or deny it their compassion,
Of that love are not possessed
Which Christ made the Christian test.

Give the poor their pittance then,
  Share with them our earthly treasures;
Heaven will yield us back again
  All our gifts in ampler measures;
Even cups of water earn
For their donors a return.

From His mansion in the skies
  When Christ came to visit mortals,
Like the poor, in humble guise,
  Did His footsteps seek their portals,
Heed, then, how we say these nay,
Lest we turn the Lord away.

"Glimpses of the Brotherhood of Charity," go forth on your mission of love! Go from the great Atlantic to the Pacific coast and make known the scenes you have portrayed. Tell all of the goodness of God, whose loving kindness ever watches over us. Tell the story of the Brothers of Charity, who have chosen that beautiful mark of the dear Christ for their title — "God is Charity."

CHAPTER VIII.

The Novitiate — The Interior Life of the Brothers of Charity.

When we come to seek the source of the wonderful power which the Brothers possess over the hearts of those whom they instruct and care for, we shall find it in the excellent training they receive during the years they spend in the novitiate. They are taught there to be men of broad sympathies, and of such tender interest in their charges, that all may see in them friends and helpers; and thus the orphan, the sick, and the afflicted respond to their interest in them with an answering love and trust.

Oftentimes this grand and noble spirit of the Brothers of Charity is subjected to severe and trying tests. The heedless and outside world

takes little or no recognition of their work; and it frequently occurs that those they have benefited most, offer nothing in return but the most bitter ingratitude. It requires no small amount of virtue to withstand such trials — yet these are the battles a Brother of this Congregation must arm himself to enter.

These exterior works and sacrifices represent, however, only one aspect of the life of a Brother of Charity. We find united with these the interior life which he leads in the Community. The world sees little or nothing of this life.

His life is indeed one of hard labor. To the foolish and thoughtless world it may seem "a stumbling block and a folly," but to us who believe in the mighty power of prayer, it becomes a sublime life and worthy of our respect and admiration. For what is it we seek for in a life worthy of admiration? Is it not the love of God and self-sacrifice?

He who lays down his life in a good cause is called a hero. His name is written in letters of gold on tablets of the most precious marble, and people call him great. Who can visit an institution conducted by the Brothers of Charity and witness their ceaseless toil from morning until night to alleviate human misery, without feeling that they are foremost in the ranks of the heroes of our age? What age ever needed them more? When were weak souls more in want of the bracing air of such examples?

But do not seek *their* history, *their* mission, or *their* work on tablets of marble or in letters of gold. You will look in vain. But ask the orphan, the sick, the unfortunate, and oppressed, and in one voice they will tell you: "I was sick, and they visited me; I was hungry, and they gave me to eat; I was naked, and they clothed me."

The man who enters the ranks of the Brothers of Charity must prepare himself for a conflict. The rules of the Congregation are such that none but he who truly denies himself and the world, for the Kingdom of Heaven's sake, can follow. They loom up before his mind day after day during his years of probation; they are read in the refectory during the meals of the Community; they are commented upon by the Superior in his conferences, so that the novice, when he reaches the time of taking his final vows which will bind him forever to the Congregation, clearly and distinctly understands the nature of the life he is about to undertake; and in case he thinks the yoke too heavy or too hard to bear, he is free to go, and the best wishes and prayers of the Community follow him. If he determines to make his vows, he becomes a full member of the Congregation; he gives up his will entirely to his Superiors.

But are there no consolations in such a life? Yes, many. They are those *spiritual* consolations that the world never knows or experiences. In such a life the soul, by constant acts of self-denial, becomes strained of grossness, and seeks its peace and happiness in God alone.

Idleness, to the Brother of Charity, is the enemy of the soul. He, therefore, upon making his vows, consecrates himself to a life of labor. No matter what a Brother's previous station in the world may have been, he must perform, according to his vow of obedience, the most menial services of the Community, if commanded by his Superior. In many of their convents the occupations of the Brothers are as various as that of a modern factory. One cannot help observing this, even in the House of The Angel Guardian, which is considered small in comparison to the other institutions under the direction of the Brothers. Among them none are exempt from work; there is no place among them for the sluggard. When it is borne in mind that their institutions are more or less self-dependant with regard to labor, the necessity for much work becomes manifest. Thus there is scope for intellects of all degrees, and talents of well-nigh every order. Daily life from year to year is an exact system of duties and hours. Their institutions, as a rule, are very large and penetrated by long corridors, which must be kept faultlessly clean. The kitchen and sometimes three or four refectories are all in charge of a Brother, with a few assistants. There is a pharmacy and infirmary; a tailor's shop where the worn garments are patched; a shoemaker's shop where the shoes are made and cobbled; and a printing office where periodicals, pamphlets, job work, etc., of all kinds are carefully printed.

Thus they labor day after day, blessing the opportunities they have of working hard, for they are taught during their years in the novitiate that labor is a blessed thing to the religious soul. It keeps the mind and body occupied, and shuts out worldly ideas. It is labor united with prayer that enables the soul to soar way beyond the gilded toys of this earth, finding no object worthy its capacities until it rests with God. The mind becomes associated with all that is elevated and pure. In such a life, free from the trappings of a foolish and deceitful world, the soul rises to its loftiest exercise, and the holy influence of all that is pure and good fills it with a joy that is unspeakable and full of glory.

The habit worn by the Brothers of Charity is simple but impressive. It consists of a long black tunic with a cincture around the waist, from which hang the beads. Over this gracefully falls a long, black scapular, which almost reaches the ground. A small, black skull-cap completes the outfit. Their diet is simple, and the table-service is of the rudest kind.

Strange, indeed, is the picture the life of a Brother of Charity presents to the nineteenth century. The agnostic may look upon it as folly, but to the eye of the Christian soul it presents a picture beautiful to look upon, because it speaks of the nothingness of the pleasures of this transitory life,— it speaks of a place in this world of sin where the soul comes to lay itself in simplicity before the Eternal as it would upon a naked, solitary rock of the desert, and offer its life as a holocaust.

To those who have the happy privilege of living among such men, life becomes sweet. Days pass, and the world and its frivolities, which are everywhere around, seem to recede to a dim remoteness, and are gradually forgotten. You are in the world, and yet not of it.

It is only when one, alive with sympathetic

interest, voluntarily enters into the history of the life of any one of these Brothers, who has passed years of service in the Master's vineyard, that he gets a glimpse of the steady fires of genuine charity that have burned all along — and then for a moment one thinks while such men exist the world is not so cruel after all—heart answers to heart, love becomes real, brotherhood becomes vital; and the weary and deserted become more precious than the highest monarch.

Living in any one of their convents one gets a pleasant infusion of actual experience with souls that are truly religious. He finds himself, for one thing, brought face to face with that life which had always existed in his dreams, and which now becomes a reality.

These are the men who hush the discordant conflict of misery by the sweet strains of charity. They have penetrated deep into the life of suffering humanity, and filled with the zeal of their vocation, they have helped many a weary little one who has come to them footsore and bleeding from the rough road of a cruel and heartless world.

* * * * * * * *

Abode of peace and home of virtue! who can judge of the life beneath thy roof save he who has lived it! Who can relate the undreamt of spiritual consolations that come even in this present life to those of thy household, save he who has experienced them? Time may erase from my mind the most cherished memories, but the heavenly consolations received within thy bosom shall never die. They will exist here like stars shining in the firmament of this dark life to cheer and brighten my path, foreshadowing the life that is to come in the mansions of the blessed.

APPENDIX.

One of the recent intentions proposed by our Holy Father to the members of the Apostleship of Prayer, that pious organization which daily petitions the Throne of Grace for the relief of the pressing needs of the Church universal, was that they should particularly ask from Heaven the boon of more numerous vocations to the religious orders and societies, which, as Leo XIII. is well aware, are often hampered in the good works they seek to perform by the lack of co-laborers in their beneficent and noble undertakings. The words which the Divine Founder of Christianity, while He was here on earth, addressed to His followers when He told them that "the harvest was, indeed great, but the workmen were few in number," are applicable to the various fields which the

Church is endeavoring to cultivate to-day; and there is not a single one of our religious orders, congregations, societies, brotherhoods, and sisterhoods toiling in those fields, that would not be able to secure far greater success in its respective labors, could it command more co-operators in the work in which it is especially engaged.

In the preceding chapters the author of this work has striven, and not wholly without success he trusts, to make known the exalted and benevolent character of the congregation to which these devoted Christian workers belong, and to give some idea of the nature of the labors which engross their days and their best endeavors. The incalculable amount of good which the Brothers of Charity have wrought, and are still doing, in the several fields of their labor, cannot fail to have impressed the reader; neither can the fact have escaped attention that the results of their toils might readily have been attended with still greater benefits to their charges were the congregation able to command the services of a more numerous membership at their different houses.

No persons can be more convinced of the truth of this assertion than are the good Brothers themselves, and, consequently, one of their fondest desires, and one for which they pray most fervently and frequently, is that the Master whom they seek to serve will send more laborers into the vineyards which are committed to their care; in other words, that vocations to become Brothers of Charity may be more numerously given to Catholic young men.

If, therefore, this book comes into the hands of any young man who, after reading its story of the Brothers of Charity and their works, is sensible of a desire within him of joining that noble band of Christian toilers and participating in their benevolent and noble labors, let him not disregard what may be the voice of Heaven calling upon him as Christ called upon His disciples to follow Him. Let him look upon himself as an especially honored person, since he is called, as it were, to do the very work which Christ Himself loved to perform, and to labor for the poor and needy of that class of whom He said: "Suffer little children to come unto Me, and forbid them not, for of such is the Kingdom of Heaven."

The Catholic youth, then, who is conscious of a desire to share in the labors and rewards of the life of a Brother of Charity, should hasten to consult with some member of the Congregation as to the best way of satisfying that desire. Application to any of the Houses of the Brotherhood will furnish him with that enlightenment, and if he has a vocation to join the Congregation, his coming will be hailed with welcome, for none are more desirous than the good Brothers themselves of seeing their ranks increased, so that they may be able to carry out more completely the grand design of their noble congregation.

HOUSE OF THE ANGEL GUARDIAN,

- - - CONDUCTED BY THE - - -

BROTHERS * OF * CHARITY.

THIS is an Institution where Orphan, Homeless, and Wayward boys receive shelter, food, and clothing, are instructed in the principles of our Holy Faith, and afterwards provided with suitable homes in good Catholic families, or taught some useful trade whereby they may earn an honest livelihood after leaving the Institution. The House, having no regular income, depends almost entirely upon the charitable public for support. Its main resource is the

Society of the Angel Guardian.

Established in 1854 by the Rev. GEORGE F. HASKINS, under the Presidency of the Most Rev. JOHN J. WILLIAMS, Archbishop of Boston, it has received the approval of Pope Pius IX. and also of Pope Leo XIII., who is a life member. Its object is to provide for poor, orphan, or abandoned children. All subscriptions and donations are applied exclusively to this work. The Society is also an association of prayer, each member being expected to recite each day the prayers printed on his card, and so obtain the indulgences attached thereto.

Special Advantages of the Society.

MASSES.— A DAILY MASS for all members; a WEEKLY MASS for collectors and life members; a WEEKLY MASS in petition for the special favors requested through the prayers of the Society; TWO HUNDRED ANNUAL MASSES for deceased members; a SPECIAL MASS OF REQUIEM for each member at death, due notice of the same being given to the Treasurer.

INDULGENCES.— Granted by Pope Pius IX.: A Plenary Indulgence on the day of admission; a Plenary Indulgence each year, Oct. 2, Feast of the Angel Guardian; a Plenary Indulgence at the hour of death; an Indulgence of three hundred days as often as members shall recite the Pater, Ave, and Gloria

Patri, in honor of the Angel Guardian. Granted by Pope Leo XIII.: A Plenary Indulgence each year, Dec. 8, Feast of the Immaculate Conception, to Collectors of the Society; an Indulgence of fifty days, once a day, to all within the Archdiocese of Boston who devoutly recite the Prayers on membership card; an Indulgence of one hundred days, likewise once a day, to all who devoutly recite said Prayers and perform some good work for the Poor or our Orphans; a Plenary Indulgence once a year, a day at their choice, to all who, both by the daily recital of said prayers and by an annual performance of some good work, shall have aided in maintaining and educating, in a Catholic manner, the Poor and Orphans, provided, however, that they receive worthily the sacraments of Penance and Holy Eucharist, visit the Parochial Church, and there pray for the intentions of His Holiness.

PRAYERS.— The children and the Brothers, generally numbering over three hundred souls, make special petitions to the Throne of Mercy twice daily, in behalf of their benefactors.

Members and Collectors.

The title of COLLECTOR is given to all who receive and forward subscriptions for the Society. "Life-Members" share in all the benefits of the Society after death, so long as their souls need prayer. Friends and deceased persons may be enrolled as members, by sending their names with the subscription fee.

Subscriptions.

A yearly Membership Card will be transmitted for self or friends, living or deceased, on receipt of TWENTY-FIVE CENTS.

A Life-membership Card will be transmitted on receipt of TEN DOLLARS. Life-membership Cards will also be given to any person collecting and forwarding ten dollars with subscribers' name.

PREMIUMS.— Each time collectors or other persons forward ten dollars in one or more payments within the space of a year, they may have their choice of the following premiums:— A Gilt Prayer Book; the "Pictorial Lives of the Saints," richly gilt and a most beautiful book; "Christ and His Church," a beautiful, richly gilt edition, prepared expressly for us; a Catholic Book or Chromo, as they may select, or two gold crosses. For five dollars, one gold cross.

All members and friends of the Orphans are entreated to earnestly endeavor to extend the Society by distributing circulars among their friends and neighbors, pointing out to them the increased Spiritual Advantages thereof, remembering that every little helps, and that whatever they do will be amply rewarded by Him who has promised that "Even a cup of cold water given in My Name has its reward."

THE ORPHAN'S FRIEND.

For the Society of the Angel Guardian.

This is a Quarterly Family Paper, Published with the Approbation of the

MOST REVEREND JOHN J. WILLIAMS,

Archbishop of Boston,

For the exclusive benefit of the orphans and destitute or abandoned children in the House of the Angel Guardian. In the seventh year of its existence, it is now a resource only second in importance to the SOCIETY OF THE ANGEL GUARDIAN. Without it the House could but very inadequately meet its demands. A constant and unremitting effort has been made to render it a paper that can be read with benefit in Catholic homes. Its contents are almost wholly original, the contribuors including some of our best Catholic writers. *The Orphan's Friend* Stories, contributed by subscribers or members of the Society in competition for prizes, a feature recently adopted, will be found most interesting. It is printed in our Industrial School by the boys of the House.

Subscribers, at the same time that they are procuring a firstrate paper for home reading, have also the satisfaction of knowing that their subscriptions aid the noble charity for which the House was founded, and entitle them to all the privileges of membership in the Society of the Angel Guardian.

The annual subscription is only 25 cents. With the receipt therefor a yearly card of membership in the Society is also sent when requested.

All persons sending a club of forty subscribers at above rates, are registered Life-members of the Society, and receive in addition a desirable premium.

Collectors helping to extend the circulation of *The Orphan's Friend* can have the paper sent direct by mail to club subscribers as well as to individual subscribers.

The Orphan's Friend is also published in the French language. Any of our readers desiring the French copy will please apply to the House of the Angel Guardian.

When writing, name Town, County, and State. Subscriptions should be sent by Post-office or Registered Letter to insure safe arrival. Address,

BROTHER JUDE, Treasurer,
85 Vernon Street, Boston, Mass.

The Orphan's Bouquet,

T. A. DWYER, A. B., Editor.

A Charming, Instructive, and Entertaining Catholic Story Paper,

- - - PUBLISHED BY THE - - -

BROTHERS OF CHARITY,

House of the Angel Guardian, 85 Vernon Street, Boston, Mass.

The public is no doubt already acquainted with our Catholic publication, titled THE ORPHAN'S BOUQUET. But, in order to advance its circulation, we ask you to kindly give this matter your attention; and after learning the object of the journal, we earnestly ask your co-operation in its advancement.

THE ORPHAN'S BOUQUET was established by Brother Jude, Superior of the House of the Angel Guardian, with the view of giving the boys of the Institution an opportunity to learn the printing trade. God has blessed the work. During the past year the success of the journal has been marvellous. But we feel that were its merits, as a Catholic story paper, more widely known, the success would be much greater, and the proceeds increased, in a way, to help the good Brothers advance their great work in the cause of orphanage.

Our children and young people must read something; and if not supplied with good wholesome reading, they will patronize the trashy novels and journals to be had at all our bookstalls. Unless something is done to prevent the reading of this vile literature by our young people, it will go on increasing in volume and repulsiveness until it is violently done away with by some decree of the Almighty, enforced in an effectual manner by bold and fearless reformers.

There can be no healthy or reliable literature which has not for its object to elevate and ennoble the mind of youth, and lead all who read it to become good Christians and upright citizens. We shall do the utmost in our power to bring about this good result.

This being the well understood position which we sincerely have taken, determined to adhere to it in the face of all discouragements, it remains with the clergy and people whether or not our journal will be the great success we hope it to be. We need a large financial backing to enable us to do pleasantly the great and good work we are ambitious to do; namely, the planting of virtue and goodness in all hearts, the inspiring of a love for our parochial schools, and soliciting the interest of all in their advancement. We intend to do this in the spirit of peacefulness and confidence, rather than in those ways which lead only to discord, wretchedness and ruin.

Send us your name and address, or the name and address of any friend whom you wish to receive a specimen copy of THE ORPHAN'S BOUQUET.

RATES.— Single copies, 5 cents; subscription for one year, $1.25. Special terms to Pastors, Teachers, Agents, School Clubs, and Societies.

OPINIONS OF NOTABLE WRITERS.

From Bro. Azarias.
Author of "The Philosophy of English Literature," etc.

DE SALLE INSTITUTE, March 3, 1892.

DEAR BRO. JUDE,—After perusing several copies of THE ORPHAN'S BOUQUET, I must say I found pleasure and instruction in them. The little journal is well edited and neatly gotten up. It is a credit to the House of the Angel Guardian. I can only say complimentary things of it, and I hope it is meeting with the success it deserves.

Believe me, very sincerely yours, BRO. AZARIAS.

From the Most Rev. W. H. Elder, D. D.

BROTHER JUDE. CINCINNATI, OHIO, March 9, 1892.

ESTEEMED BROTHER,—His Grace, Archbishop Elder, would have me express his good wishes for you and all your house, and as a token of the interest he feels in the good work you are doing, he has instructed me to send his subscription for the coming year. I am, with respectful regard,

Your obedient servant, REV. MICHAEL AHERN.

From Rt. Rev. D. M. Bradley, D. D.

MANCHESTER, N. H., March 9, 1892,

REV. AND DEAR BRO. JUDE,—I am very willing to allow my name to be added to the list of those who have written words of approval of your publication—THE ORPHAN'S BOUQUET. I have read copies of it from time to time and am pleased to say that I have always regarded it as a very commendable Catholic family journal. Yours respectfully,

✠ DENIS M. BRADLEY, Bishop of Manchester.

From Very Rev. Wm. Byrne, D. D., V. G.

ST. JOSEPH'S CHURCH, BOSTON, March 11, 1892.

EDITOR ORPHAN'S BOUQUET,—I have examined several numbers of THE ORPHAN'S BOUQUET, and think well of it. It is interesting and instructive. The mechanical work is a credit to your printing office. The boys engaged in it will know at least one trade well. Yours truly, WILLIAM BYRNE, V. G.

From Rev. Charles W. Currier.
Author of "The Carmelites in America."

WALDORF, March 4, 1892.

THOS. A. DWYER, ESQ., Boston.

Dear Sir,—I received with great pleasure the copies of THE ORPHAN'S BOUQUET you kindly forwarded to me. There are especially two features in the bright periodical which have impressed me — its originality and its spirit of enterprise. Most of your articles are written for THE ORPHAN'S BOUQUET, and you bravely solicit agents all over the country to advance the worthy periodical. It is certainly the way to success. You have a notice to your advertisers which reads thus: "We propose that the advertising columns of THE ORPHAN'S BOUQUET shall be as pure and wholesome as its reading columns." Bravo! This ought to be copied by every Catholic paper in the country. Wishing you every possible success,

I remain, yours, CHARLES W. CURRIER.

From Rev. J. Nilan, D. D.

POUGHKEEPSIE, N. Y.

EDITOR OF THE ORPHAN'S BOUQUET.

Dear Sir,— Your tasteful publication is always a welcome visitor. Its utility is undoubted, for it contains many valuable moral as well as scientific articles. Its decent tone, free from anything that can give offence to our Christian brethren outside the fold, ought to be adopted by all periodicals bearing the holy name of Catholic. It has also fallen creditably in line with the other reputable publications that have either excluded or removed from their advertising columns the liquor business, so reprobated by the Council of Baltimore. Your city is singularly favored in having such eminent Catholic writers and scholars, who bring credit to the Church. May God's law of progress guide you onwards. Yours, etc., J. NILAN.

From W. D. Kelly.

DORCHESTER, March 10, 1892.

DEAR MR. DWYER,— I gladly certify to the literary excellence and high merits of THE ORPHAN'S BOUQUET, which, I think, is filling a field hitherto unoccupied by Catholic journalism hereabouts, and the good of whose influence is incalculable.

W. D. KELLY.

From Bishop Brooks.

233 CLARENDON ST., BOSTON, Oct. 12, 1892.

MY DEAR MR. DWYER,— You have infused into THE BOUQUET a spirit that must do good. Never shall I cease to thank you for your goodness in sending me a copy each week. Allow me to express my cordial sympathy with the great work THE BOUQUET is destined to do, and my thankfulness for the success which is attending it. I am,

Yours most sincerely, PHILLIPS BROOKS.

From Rev. Francis J. Finn, S. J.
Author of "Tom Playfair" and "Percy Wynn."

T. A. DWYER,   WOODSTOCK COLLEGE.

Dear Sir,—The improvement you are making each week in THE ORPHAN'S BOUQUET is amazing. With best wishes for your success, I remain,   Yours in Christ,
                                        FRANCIS J. FINN, S. J.

From George Parsons Lathrop.

                              NEW LONDON, April 14, 1893.

MY DEAR MR. DWYER,—THE BOUQUET will certainly do a great deal of good in the field of literature. I am glad to see so many eminent Catholic writers among its contributors.

     Very sincerely yours, GEORGE PARSONS LATHROP.

From Rev. A. P. Doyle, C. S. P.
Editor of the *Catholic World*.

                                  NEW YORK, Feb. 28, 1893.

MY DEAR MR. DWYER,—Allow me to congratulate you on the energy and push you have infused into THE ORPHAN'S BOUQUET, and the high standard you have achieved.
                     Sincerely yours,   A. P. DOYLE.

OPINIONS OF THE PRESS.

"THE ORPHAN'S BOUQUET, which is printed and published by the House of the Angel Guardian, at 85 Vernon Street, is an illustrated weekly for young readers which is increasing rapidly in influence and circulation. Its editor, Mr. T. A. Dwyer, is a progressive and enterprising journalist, who has improved the paper greatly since it came under his supervision. THE BOUQUET has recently been enlarged, and is full of sweetness and light."—*Boston Saturday Evening Gazette.*

"THE ORPHAN'S BOUQUET, which is published at the House of the Angel Guardian, has been increased to sixteen pages. This is a great mark of appreciation. We congratulate our young contemporary on its success."—*Boston Pilot.*

"THE ORPHAN'S BOUQUET, a weekly family paper, first issued by the House of the Angel Guardian, Jan. 1, 1891, has been quietly making its way into favor. Neat and modest in appearance, its contents are of unusual merit. Well written original stories constitute the greater part of its make-up. But able articles on eminent topics are frequently given."—*Boston Daily Globe.*

"The new frontispiece makes a decided improvement in the appearance of THE ORPHAN'S BOUQUET. Although only in its second year, it has already won an enviable place in the list of weekly Catholic story papers by the excellence of its stories and illustrations. The tone of the reading matter, which, by the way, is originally written for this paper, is above the ordinary. THE ORPHAN'S BOUQUET is printed and published in Boston, at the House of the Angel Guardian, an institution for homeless or destitute boys, conducted by the Brothers of Christian Charity, and is sold at $1.25 a year."—*Annals of Our Lady of the Sacred Heart.*

"One of the brightest and purest periodicals that comes to our table is THE ORPHAN'S BOUQUET. It is really a charming publication, and ought to be in every Catholic household."—*Catholic Sentinel, Chippewa Falls, Wis.*

"THE ORPHAN'S BOUQUET, published by the House of the Angel Guardian, Boston, Mass., is on our table. It is superbly illustrated, and its typographical appearance is equal to the best. The matter excellent, and being principally original throughout, it is most creditable to the publishers, and should have a large circulation on its intrinsic merits as well as for the noble work it is aiding and doing. Subscription price $1.25 per year."—*Kansas Catholic.*

www.ingramcontent.com/pod-product-compliance
Lightning Source LLC
Chambersburg PA
CBHW020933230426
43666CB00008B/1668